THE AUTHORS

Jill Foster has been a literary agent for over 20 years and has run her own agency for most of that time.

Malcolm Hamer worked in marketing for various multinational companies and then formed his own agency to represent sportsmen and television journalists. He has also written nearly 30 books, including six novels.

They live in London with their daughter, Polly, who started it all.

THE
FAMILY WELCOME GUIDE

To Hotels, Pubs,
Restaurants and
Self-Catering
For All The Family

First published in Great Britain in 1999 by
POOLSIDE PUBLISHING

10 9 8 7 6 5 4 3 2 1

While every attempt has been made to ensure accuracy
throughout the book, the nature of the travel business is such
that the authors and publishers cannot be held liable for changes
which occur after the time of writing.

ISBN 0 95282 592 9

Typeset by Words That Work Limited
Underriver, Kent TN15 0SJ
Tel: 01732 838994
Printed and bound in Finland by
Werner Söderström Osakeyhtiö
Distributed by Portfolio,
Unit 1C, West Ealing Business Centre
Alexandria Road
London W13 0NJ
Tel: 020 8579 7748

POOLSIDE PUBLISHING
3 Lonsdale Road
London SW13 9ED

PREDATOR

A novel of power and corruption and the ruthless
business of sport

By

Malcolm Hamer

Out in paperback now at £6.99

CONTENTS

*The front cover photograph is of the
Old Bell Hotel, Malmesbury, by kind
permission of the owners.*

THE GOOD HOLIDAY COTTAGE GUIDE

If you like the philosophy of the *Family Welcome Guide* (we certainly do), then you will probably also appreciate *The Good Holiday Cottage Guide*. It too is critical, highly selective and based exclusively on first hand visits. The Guide deals only with self-catering properties throughout the UK, with a handful of favourites in Ireland, and in fifteen years of its existence (it is published annually) it has become essential reading for the many people who enjoy the freedom and independence holiday cottages, apartments and chalets offer.

The Guide covers all the UK, plus a few favourites in the south of Ireland. It is strong on East Anglia, Yorkshire, Northumberland, Scotland, Cumbria and the Lake District, Wales, the West Country, the south east of England and the Cotswolds. Every property featured has been visited by a small team of editors, and certain features are identified. For experience shows readers of the Guide particularly like to know about cottages on working farms, with animals to fuss over, cottages where home cooked food is available, cottages with open fires and/or wood burning stoves, cottages that are by the sea or overlook a lake or loch. They want information about swimming pools, snooker tables and tennis courts. (The latter are regarded as a luxury, and owners say a hard tennis court has a greater appeal than an open air pool.) Always popular are panoramic views, especially from bedrooms, thatched roofs, antique furniture, large houses that sleep two or more families and – always – properties that take dogs.

Published each January, *The Good Holiday Cottage Guide*, is unique. It is almost a 'labour of love' for its editors, and essential reading for serious cottage fanciers. It has about 450 pages, including colour sections, and is well illustrated. It costs £5.95 from bookshops and newsagents or, in case of difficulty, for the same price from Swallow Press, PO Box 21, Hertford, Herts. SG14 2DD (01438 869489). Like the Family Welcome Guide, it is distributed by Portfolio, Unit 1C West Ealing Business Centre, London W13 0NJ. Telephone 020 8579 7748.

INTRODUCTION

The first edition of *THE FAMILY WELCOME GUIDE* was published in 1984, when, with some rare exceptions, hoteliers, publicans and restaurateurs regarded families with children with unequivocal distaste: the usual order of the day was "They shall not pass". Our objective, when we began our research in the early 80s, was to unearth places where families with children were treated like normal human beings. And we succeeded; and we are delighted that a goodly proportion of the enlightened establishments recommended in that first edition is still to be found in these pages.

As in all our previous editions the hotels, pubs, restaurants and self-catering establishments we recommend are an exclusive band which not only offer excellent facilites for families but also something intangible and invaluable - a warm welcome.

Our hotels range from simple farmhouses with a few rooms to splendid seaside and country hotels with a full range of amenities. What they have in common are the basic facilities which families need: cots and high chairs and a free baby listening service. And a great deal more – a real and friendly welcome for a start. Many of them have an array of extras which add immensely to their guests' fun: swimming pools, play areas, tennis and squash courts, fishing and even golf courses. The self-catering establishments in the guide mirror these facilities. It should also be noted that many of the pubs and restaurants we recommend have accommodation and we mention this when appropriate.

THE ENTRIES
We try to present the information in the simplest form, without any of those confusing codes or symbols.

Name of the town or village, and its county or region.
Name of the establishment, and whether it is an **hotel** Ⓗ, a **pub** Ⓟ, a **restaurant** Ⓡ or as **self-catering accomodation** Ⓢ. Sometimes establishments are entered in more than one category.

Directions. These should enable you to find your way to the front door – but all hotels and self-catering places provide detailed maps and directions.

Description: we try to give you an impression of what the place is like and why we have included it and we summarize its facilities.

Food: we give you the serving times, and an idea of the price range and (if possible) type of food on offer. For restaurant meals (as opposed to bar snacks) we quote the price of a three-course meal and sometimes an extract from a typical menu. Since prices are hard to forecast we have quoted to the nearest £, and have rounded figures upward. We tell you if special menus or smaller portions are available for children.

Opening and closing times except for pubs which are usually open throughout the day every day of the year, with the exception of Christmas Day.

Ale means real ale and we name the brands available.

Hotel information includes:

Price of rooms: In general we give the 'Best Room Rate' ie. the lowest bed and breakfast price (for one person) quoted by the hotel – but you should always check the price carefully before booking.

Best Bargain Break: every hotel offers bargain breaks, especially at weekends, and we have given these prices when they are available. There are great advantages in hunting these breaks out, since they really are bargains, especially out of season.

Children: we give you the terms for children and these are always on the basis that a child is sharing a room with its parents.

Facilities: we tell you how many cots and high chairs are available, and to what extent a baby-listening service is offered.

Number of rooms: we give the total number of rooms in hotels, and the number of family rooms (ie, which can sleep ar least three people). We also mention suites, and interconnecting rooms. Apart from these, most hotels have other rooms which will take cots and/or extra beds.

We are writing this introduction in October, 1999. We have made every effort to check the facts in our reports – invariably with the help of the management of each establishment recommended. However, managements change and prices are altered. We cannot be held responsible for changes which are made after we have gone to press. We repeat that it is essential, therefore, that you check basic information, such as the cost of accommodation, before you book.

For the first seven or eight years of the *FAMILY WELCOME GUIDE*'s existence, we did not accept any fees for inclusion in the guide. We then changed our policy and, along with many other guidebooks, invited the places we recommended to pay a modest subscription to cover our research costs. The AA has a similar practice.

We must stress that such payments have never affected our objectivity; no hotel, pub or restaurant has ever bought its way into our guides. Every potential entry is inspected and, if our various stern criteria are met, the owner is invited to participate in the guide – on our terms since every report is written by us. No promotional hyperbole finds its way into *THE FAMILY WELCOME GUIDE*.

All the places in the guide are re-inspected on a regular basis and if their standards drop they are excluded. We give serious weight to the comments of our readers and thank all those people who have written to us.

In keeping with the technological spirit of the Millennium, the *Guide* now has a website. It is registered as:

www.familywelcomeguide.co.uk

and you will find information there about some of the establishments we recommend. Many of them have their own dedicated websites which you can hotkey.

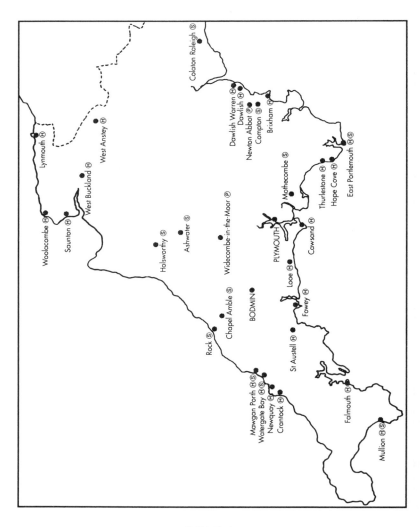

MAP 1
WEST OF ENGLAND

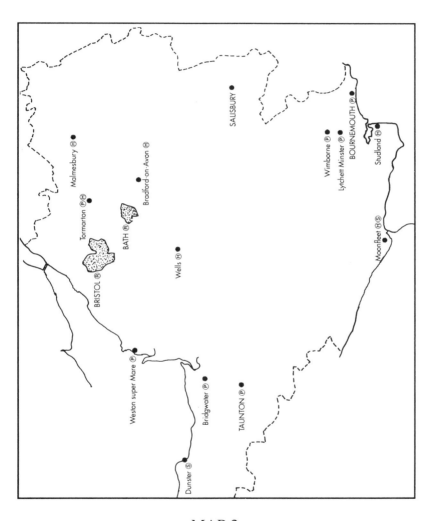

MAP 2
MID-WEST ENGLAND

THE FAMILY WELCOME GUIDE

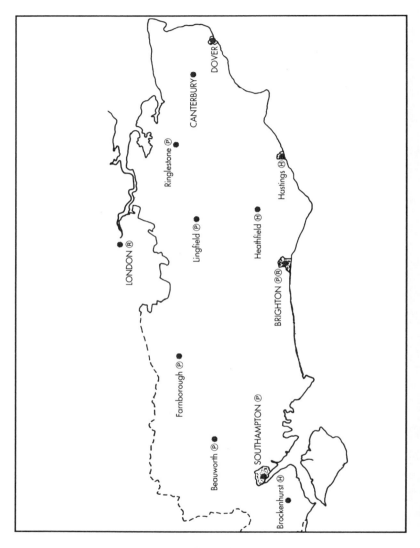

DOVER ●●

CANTERBURY ●

Ringlestone ℗ ●

Hastings Ⓗ ●●

Heathfield Ⓗ ●

LONDON Ⓡ ●

Lingfield ℗ ●

BRIGHTON ℗Ⓡ ●●

Farnborough ℗ ●

Beauworth ℗ ●

SOUTHAMPTON ℗ ●

Brockenhurst Ⓗ ●

MAP 3
LONDON, SOUTH and SOUTH-EAST ENGLAND

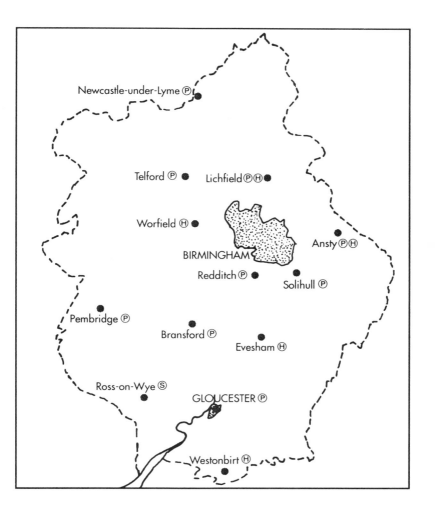

Newcastle-under-Lyme ⓟ

Telford ⓟ   Lichfield ⓟⒽ

Worfield Ⓗ

BIRMINGHAM

Ansty ⓟⒽ

Redditch ⓟ

Solihull ⓟ

Pembridge ⓟ

Bransford ⓟ

Evesham Ⓗ

Ross-on-Wye Ⓢ

GLOUCESTER ⓟ

Westonbirt Ⓗ

MAP 4
HEART of ENGLAND

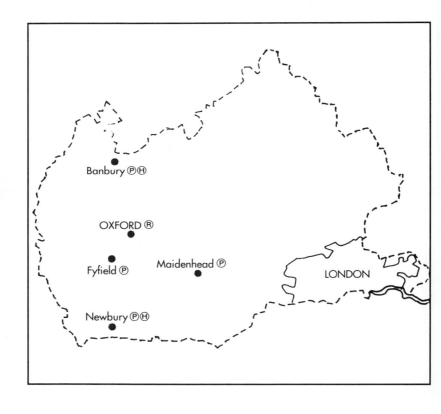

Banbury ⓅⒽ

OXFORD ⓇⒶ

Fyfield Ⓟ

Maidenhead Ⓟ

LONDON

Newbury ⓅⒽ

MAP 5
THAMES and CHILTERNS

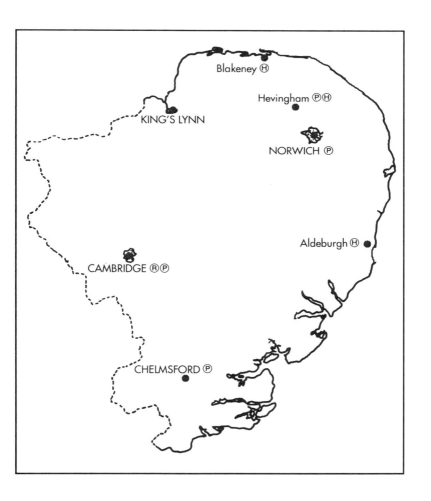

Blakeney Ⓗ

Hevingham ⓅⒽ

KING'S LYNN

NORWICH Ⓟ

Aldeburgh Ⓗ

CAMBRIDGE ⓇⓅ

CHELMSFORD Ⓟ

MAP 6
EAST of ENGLAND

MAP 7
EAST MIDLANDS

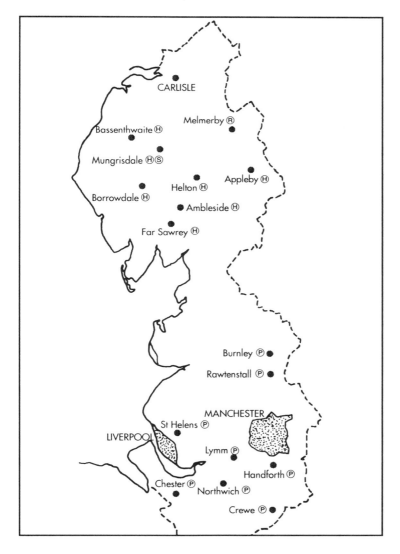

CARLISLE

Melmerby ®

Bassenthwaite ⓗ

Mungrisdale ⓗⓢ

Appleby ⓗ

Helton ⓗ

Borrowdale ⓗ

Ambleside ⓗ

Far Sawrey ⓗ

Burnley ⓟ ●

Rawtenstall ⓟ ●

MANCHESTER

St Helens ⓟ

LIVERPOOL

Lymm ⓟ

Handforth ⓟ

Chester ⓟ

Northwich ⓟ

Crewe ⓟ ●

MAP 8
NORTH-WEST ENGLAND

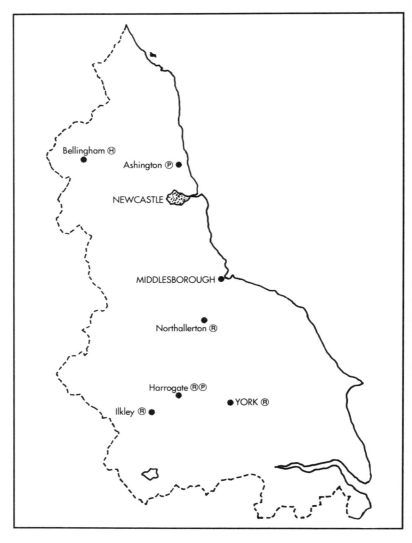

Bellingham Ⓗ

Ashington Ⓟ

NEWCASTLE

MIDDLESBOROUGH

Northallerton Ⓡ

Harrogate ⓇⓅ

Ilkley Ⓡ

YORK Ⓡ

MAP 9
NORTH-EAST ENGLAND

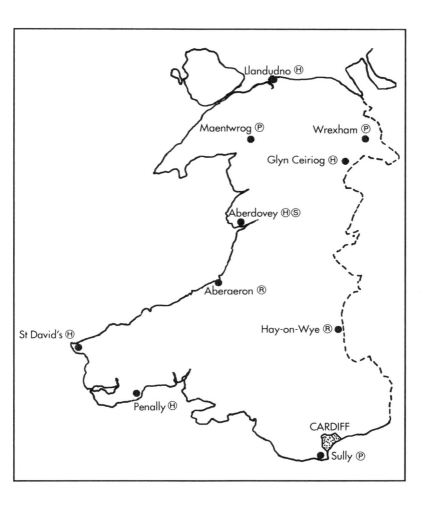

MAP 10
WALES

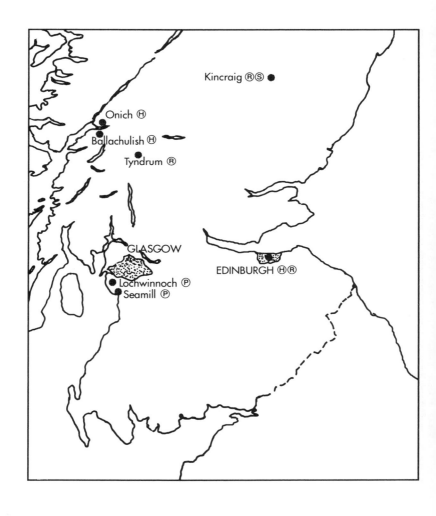

MAP 11
SCOTLAND

ENGLAND

ALDEBURGH, SUFFOLK   Map 6
⊞ WENTWORTH HOTEL, Wentworth Road
Tel: 01728 452 312
Next to the beach, near the town centre

....

This very appealing hotel has a splendid position overlooking the sea across a pebbled beach, where the fishermen still sell their catch in the morning. Many of the bedrooms have lovely views, as have the attractive restaurant and the sun room, which is a delightful spot in which to relax. The main lounge is alongside, an elegant room with comfortable sofas and some good antique furniture; there is a reading room cum library on the ground floor; and the signed Russell Flint prints also add to the hotel's appeal.

On one side of the hotel there is a sunken terrace and it is a sun trap on warmer days; on the other side is a small lawned garden. The wide expanses of sea and beach lie before you and you can walk for miles in either direction.

Although there are no permanent family rooms here, eighteen of the bedrooms can be set up to take two adults and a child.

Nearby: Although the beach is shingle, Aldeburgh lies on the Suffolk coastal path which runs from Felixstowe to Lowestoft. Just to the north you can visit Minsmere Nature Reserve and the interesting village of Dunwich with its museum. A music festival is held every June at Snape Maltings and there are castles at Orford and Framlingham. Adults with an interest in wine might try visits to Brandeston Priory and Bruisyard Wines.

....

✕   Bar lunch (12pm to 2pm) £3-12: prawn and avocado salad, cod and chips, sausages and mash, fillet steak, mixed seafood casserole;
Dinner (7pm to 9pm) £15: local seafood terrine, braised knuckle of lamb, nutmeg creme brulée
Children: high teas, half portions
Best Room Rate: from £50 per person
✔   Best Bargain Break: £105 per person, 2 nights - dinner, b&b
Children: free to age 2; £10 thereafter

1

Facilities: 2 cots and 2 high chairs; 6 z-beds; baby-listening system

37 rooms

Closed 2 weeks after Christmas

♚ Ale: Adnams

🅿 Own car park and on street

AMBLESIDE, CUMBRIA   Map 8
Ⓗ ROTHAY MANOR HOTEL
Tel: 015394 33605

A few hundred yards out of the town on the Coniston Road

This elegant Regency-style hotel was once the home of a prosperous Liverpool merchant and has a distinct colonial look. The wide windows and terrace on the ground floor overlook the immaculate garden with a fine variety of trees and a rockery; on the first floor there is a veranda with iron railings. Climbing plants and hanging baskets of flowers add to the attractions.

The hotel has been in the care of the same family since 1967 and many antiques have been collected during that time to adorn the main rooms. The restaurant is non-smoking and so is one of the lounges.

The bedrooms are all individually furnished to a very high standard. Three suites are available in the grounds of the hotel, two of which are ideal for families. They are spacious and beautifully furnished and each has one double and one twin bedroom. An adjoining single room can be used by either suite and they have little terraces and enclosed gardens of their own.

Residents have free use of a nearby leisure club (one mile away) with swimming pool, sauna, steam room and jacuzzi. Squash is also available. During the winter the hotel offers music, bridge, art and antiques, painting and gardening courses.

The hotel has an excellent reputation for its food which is freshly cooked from local produce. It is a delightful place to stay in a splendid part of the Lake District.

Nearby: The hotel is situated in the heart of the Lake District with all its attractions. Fishing, golf, riding and water sports are readily available. Brockhole Visitor Centre, the Steam Boat Museum, Sizergh Castle, Levens Hall, Brantwood, the Beatrix Potter Exhibition, Fell Foot Park, Grizedale Forest Centre and the Ravenglass and Eskdale Railway (the 'Ratty') are all within easy reach.

✕   Lunch (12.30pm to 2pm) £5-13: hot dishes, sandwiches; Dinner (7.45pm to 9pm), £27: orange and grapefruit segments with a pineapple and Grand Marnier sabayon, duck breast with spicy peaches and Port and Madeira jus, vanilla and raspberry mille-feuille
Children: high teas, half portions
Best Room Rate: £61 per person

✔   Best Bargain Break: £75 per person per night - dinner, b&b
Children: free up to 10; £10 from 10 - 18
Facilities: 4 cots and 3 high chairs; baby listening
18 rooms, 5 family, 2 suites
Open early Feb to early Jan

🅿   Own car park

ANSTY, COVENTRY   Map 4
℗ ⊕ ANSTY ARMS
Tel: 01203 611 817

From junction 2 of the M6 go through Ansty on B4065. Turn right on to the B4029 and then right again.

This is a very large family pub located near the network of motorways and close to the National Exhibition Centre. It's a modern brick structure and the conservatory and the large windows ensure the interior is light and bright. That goes for the decor, too, which is lively and cheerful with patterned wallpaper, colourful lights and canopied ceilings.

The bar area is sensibly divided into various alcoves, and French windows overlook some garden greenery. The sizeable dining area has a high-domed conservatory and, above the ground floor, there is more seating in a gallery around the first floor. The family dining area has high chairs and baby-changing facilities are available.

The garden has plenty of bench seating and an excellent play area; the children will also be at home in Adventure Island, an indoor play centre with all sorts of rides, slides and ball ponds. It is supervised and has a snack and drinks bar.

The Lodge has 28 bedrooms, many of which can accommodate a family. The prices (£45.50 per room and £39.50 at weekends) are reasonable.

✕   Food (12 to 9.30pm, Sunday to Thursday; until 10pm at weekends) £2-9: home-made fish and chips, cajun chicken, prawn platter, steak
        Children: own menu

⛫   Ale: Bass, Tetley

4

APPLEBY, CUMBRIA   **Map 8**
Ⓗ **APPLEBY MANOR HOTEL**
Tel: 017683 51571
Off the A66. Follow the signs to the hotel.

This imposing manor house, made of rose-coloured Westmorland stone, overlooks the village of Appleby and the castle. The hotel was extended a few years back and is an excellent mix of old and new, and there is a notable pitch-pine staircase in the hall. The attractive public rooms include a delightful conservatory, a stately and elegant sitting room, a pleasant bar and a light and airy dining room, all with wonderful views over the gardens to Appleby and the distant hills.

The same views will delight the eye from the splendid gardens which are shaded by some fine old trees. Other facilities include the games room, which has pool and table tennis, and the leisure club, which has a plunge pool, sauna, jacuzzi, solarium and some exercise machines.

The family bedrooms are well designed and offer plenty of space; four of them have either double or twin beds and bunk beds, and the others have various combinations of four-poster, double and single beds.

With the nine family rooms, the interconnected rooms, a good supply of cots and high chairs and the excellent all-round facilities, this is a first-class family hotel and a good base for exploring this part of England.

Nearby: there is superb countryside all around, a great area for walking, fishing and riding. Golf is available in the vicinity. Appleby is a delightful town and the children will enjoy a visit to the castle. Lowther Park, with its nature trails, adventure playground and miniature railway, is close and it is easy to reach all the attractions of the Lakes and the Yorkshire Dales.

✕   Dinner (7pm to 9pm) £22: crab & prawn terrine, roast
        shoulder of pork, pudding or cheese
        Children: own menu, half portions
        Best Room Rate: £52 per person
✔   Best Bargain Break: discounts up to 20%

5

Children: free to age 15
Facilities: 6 cots and 4 high chairs; baby-listening system
30 rooms, 9 family, 4 sets interconnecting
Open all year
P Own car park

ASHINGTON, NORTHUMBERLAND   **Map 9**
℗ WOODHORN GRANGE
Tel: 01670 862 332
Off the A189 in the Queen Elizabeth II Country Park

The family pub and restaurant has a delightful location by the lake in the country park and you can sit at one of the tables outside and enjoy the view. The Woodhorn Colliery museum is on the other side of the lake and is well worth a visit.

The Woodhorn Grange is a modern stone building which offers all the facilities a family needs, including food and drink throughout the day, high chairs, a children's menu and baby changing facilities. In addition the Lodge offers rooms at a reasonable price.

The open plan interior is sensibly divided into a number of different rooms and opposite the bar are several alcoves with floor to ceiling windows which give views of the lake. The pub is nicely decked out with wood panelling, brick walls and pillars, open fireplaces and pine tables, and has old photographs on the walls. The huge L shaped dining room has Laura Ashley style wallpaper, ceiling fans and comfortable furniture. Alongside there is a Charlie Chalk Fun Factory with lots of amusements and there is a small play area for toddlers. There is also an outside play area on the patio.

✗ Food (11.30am to 10pm; from noon on Sundays) £2-8: range of hot and cold food.
Children: own menu
♀ Ale: Boddington's and guests
P Own car park

ASHWATER, DEVON   **Map 1**
ⓢ BRADDON COTTAGES

Tel: 01409 211 350.

West of Okehampton off the A30 at Roadford Lake. The brochure has clear directions.

This complex comprises six half-stone, half-cob converted barns set in nearly a hundred acres of meadow overlooking a beautiful valley with views south to Dartmoor. Alongside are fifty acres of woodland and a large fishing/boating lake. All of the units are highly original in character and are surrounded by landscaped gardens.

The six cottages are in a lovely secluded setting at the end of a long driveway. Four of them are conversions of old farm buildings and many of their original features, such as the old beams and oak floors, have been retained. They are charming places and can sleep between six and nine people plus cots. The accommodation is flexible since all of the cottages have sofa beds which can he used by larger families. All of them have patios and gardens and splendid views of the countryside.

Thc two purpose-built houses can accommodate up to thirteen people and they are also detached and have their own gardens and patios. All the houses are very well-equipped; for example, they have washing machines, dish-washers, microwaves and barbecues, as well as all the conventional items.

The excellent facilities include a games field with a swing, a slide, a sandpit, football goalposts and a hard tennis court (which also has basketball hoops). The three-acre lake is stocked with fish and has two islands with resident water birds and a boat for the guests to use. A large summer house with a barbecue is by the lake. There is a nature trail and a children's games room which has table tennis, pool, darts, board games and books. A separate room for adults has a full-size snooker table.

This is a delightful spot with splendid facilities for a family holiday in the care of the charming owners, George and Anne Ridge.

Units: 6
Rent: £90-£700 a week (bargain breaks available in winter at £60 for two people for two nights).

Cots and high chairs are available as requircd
Heating: central heating and log fires
Open all year

NR BANBURY, OXON   **Map 5**
Ⓟ Ⓗ **THE WOBBLY WHEEL**
Tel: 01295 690 214
On the B4100 south of Banbury (from junction 12 of the M40, follow the Gaydon sign).

....

This curiously named pub directs a traditional face to the world. The original building was formed of soft local stone and topped by dormer windows and a steeply-pitched roof. The original bar has stone walls and a beamed ceiling and thereafter the pub has been greatly extended. Past a stone fireplace you will find a pleasant dining area with padded settles and occasional wooden screens. Beyond is a capacious dining room, bright and cheerful under its high glass roof.

The excellent family facilities include a large lawned garden with bench seats and a sizeable play area with a safe bark surface; there is another grassy area from where you have soothing views of the countryside.

Children have their own indoor play area, Adventure Island, with a great array of ball pools, slides, mazes and so on and a sitting area. Drinks and snacks are served and staff are always present to supervise.

The Lodge has 15 bedrooms, twins or doubles which can also accommodate children in cots or z-beds and the prices are well below £50 per room (just under £40 at weekends).

....

✕   Food (12 to 9.30pm, Sunday to Thursday; until 10pm at
        weekends)£2-9: prawn platter, home-made fish & chips, cajun
        chicken, steak
        Children: own menu
♀   Ale: Bass, Boddington's, Greenall's

8

BASSENTHWAITE, nr KESWICK, CUMBRIA   **Map 8**
Ⓗ Ⓢ ARMATHWAITE HALL HOTEL
Tel: 017687 76551

Off the A591 – don't go to Bassenthwaite village but follow the brown and white tourist signs for Trotters and Friends Animal Farm

....

This is a splendid 18th-century stone building very much in the baronial style, and set in 400 acres of parkland; its lawns flow down to Bassenthwaite Lake, where guests can fish, and Skiddaw Mountain looms dramatically in the background.

Sir Hugh Walpole wrote: 'Is there anything more romantic than Armathwaite Hall. With the trees that guard it and the history that inhabits it, it is a house of perfect and irresistible atmosphere.'

There are some wonderful rooms here, including a huge lounge with a grand marble fireplace, wood-panelled ceiling and walls and leaded windows – all glassily surveyed by the stags' heads on the walls.

In addition to its beautiful situation, there are splendid facilities within the hotel: the spa has an indoor heated swimming pool, gymnasium, a hard tennis court, a pitch and putt course, and a croquet lawn. A snooker table (for over-16s) is in a remarkable panelled room with walls covered with scores of original Punch cartoons. The hotel also has an Equestrian Centre with fully qualified instructors and over twenty horses and ponies.

The hotel makes a considerable effort to look after and entertain all members of the family and, in addition to the excellent facilities mentioned above, there are special treats for the children. 'Trotters & Friends' is an animal farm park (open from April to October and at weekends in winter) with many animals to make friends with and feed. Family Treasure Hunts are held several times a week; and there are swimming galas, survival training, tennis coaching and many other activities.

Armathwaite Hall Hotel is an outstanding hotel in delightful surroundings where families will find all they need for an enjoyable stay.

There are three self-catering properties: two flats and the ground floor of the lodge. They accomodate from four to six people and the rents vary from £300 to £600 per week.

9

Nearby: From this base you can reach any part of the Lakes with ease, including Grasmere, Hardknott Roman fort, Brantwood, the Lake District headquarters at Brockhole. The children will no doubt vote for Fell Foot Park which has facilities for all types of water sports, or the Grizedale Forest Visitor Centre. Railway buffs have several choices, including the famous Ravenglass and Eskdale, known as 'La'al Ratty'.

✕ Leisure Club (12pm to 5.30pm and 7pm to 9.30pm) £2-9: garlic mushrooms, spaghetti Napoli, chicken curry, sirloin steak; Lunch (12.30pm to 1.45pm) £14: smoked salmon & cucumber salad, roast leg of pork, strawberry pavlova; Dinner (7.30pm to 9.30pm) £34: galia melon, salmon and crab ravioli, loin of lamb, pudding or cheese
Children: own menu, half portions
Best Room Rate: £ 58 per person
✔ Best Bargain Break: £168-£252 per person, 2 nights - dinner, b&b
Children: free (sharing with parents)
Facilities: 6 cots and 6 high chairs; baby-listening system for each room
42 rooms, 4 family, 2 sets interconnecting
🅿 Own car park

BATH, AVON   **Map 2**
® BROWNS RESTAURANT, Orange Grove
Tel: 01225 461 199
In the city centre.

....

The Browns group of restaurants has a policy of acquiring notable
and historic buildings and converting them into restaurants and they
have done a grand job with the Old Police House. It is a gracious old
building with a substantial stone facade and stands opposite the
grandiose Gothic splendours of the Abbey, one of the many
landmarks of this enticing city.

The cream-painted interior of the restaurant gives an immediate
impression of coolness and space, mainly because the principal room
rises high up to the roof with its several skylights. Potted plants are
dotted here and there and also hang above, amid the lazily circling
fans; and mirrors placed on the walls accentuate the feeling of
spaciousness. A grand piano is played in the early evenings. To the
rear of the restaurant the old police cells, with chilly-looking tiled
walls, form another dining area and the original door, with its forlorn
graffiti, is still in place.

As in all their establishments, Browns provide excellent facilites
for families, including plenty of high chairs, a children's menu and a
mother and baby room. We can also commend their two-course
lunch, competitively priced at £5.95.

Up the stairs you will come to the Gallery Restaurant, which has
a bar with a lounge area to one side, comfortably furnished with
padded benches and bentwood chairs. From this vantage point you
can survey the glories of the Abbey and enjoy a cocktail or two. In
addition there are tables and chairs on the pavement outside.

....

✗   Food (11am to 11.30pm; from noon on Sundays) £3-17: roast
        red peppers, salad Nicoise, venison steak, steak and
        mushroom and Guinness pie, fisherman's pie
        Children: own menu

BEAUWORTH, nr ALRESFORD, HANTS   Map 3
℗ MILBURY'S
Tel: 01962 771 248

About two miles south of the A272, and one mile beyond the hamlet of Beauworth

....

Standing alone on top of the hill, this 17th-century pub is built in soft, warm Hampshire brick with hung tiles, flint walls and dormer windows set in a many-angled roof line. It is good to report that families are welcome in various areas, so that adults can still enjoy the many real ales which are available and the excellent range of food.

A notable feature of the pub is the well in the bar. It is three hundred feet deep and an ice cube, dropped from the safety grid, takes around five seconds to hit the water. There is also a huge treadmill to be seen.

The two family rooms sit one above the other alongside the large mill wheel. There are several tables on the ground floor and up above you will find the gallery, an interesting room with a beamed sloping ceiling and wooden tables. There is also a skittle alley with several tables.

The grassy garden has superb views of the wide-open countryside. There are plenty of picnic tables, and barbecues are held during summer weekends when the pub is open throughout the day. Two swings make up a play area in a corner of the garden.

....

✕   Bar snacks (12pm to 2pm and 7pm to l0pm) £1-10: smoked salmon, cod fillet Mornay, steaks, plaice, chilli con carne
       Children: own menu, half portions

♀   Ale: Courage, King Alfred, Milbury Special, Pendragon and guests

🅿   Own car park

BELLINGHAM, nr HEXHAM, NORTHUMBERLAND   Map 9
Ⓗ RIVERDALE HALL HOTEL
Tel: 01434 220 254

On a minor road just west of Bellingham on the north bank of the River Tyne. Bellingham is on the B6320, 16 miles north of Hexham.

The core of the hotel is a Victorian country house which overlooks the North Tyne River. It is near to Kielder Water and has recently undergone a major programme of refurbishment. It has excellent facilities which include an indoor swimming pool and a games room.

The owner is a cricket enthusiast and has his own cricket field which also doubles for other sports. There is a putting green, croquet and petanque; you can fish in the adjoining river for salmon and trout and the golf course lies opposite. So sports fans are well catered for. Alternatively you can simply relax in the five acres of garden; from the terrace you have splendid views over the cricket ground to the hills beyond. The same views will also please you from the stately bar, the lounge and the pleasant dining room. The bedrooms are very well turned out and we were impressed by a spacious family room which has a four-poster bed and a single bed.

Nearby: Kielder Water, with its wide variety of water sports, can be enjoyed by the whole family; and the castle is the starting point for many walks and nature trails through the Kielder Forest. To the south you can follow the line of Hadrian's Wall with its chain of forts. Within easy reach you will find Belsay Hall, Wallington House, Cragside House and the ruins of Brinkburn Priory.

✕   Bar snacks (12pm to 2pm) £2-11: garlic mushrooms, steaks, tuna & Brie bake, vegetable curry
Dinner (6.45pm to 9.30pm) £20: devilled whitebait, mushroom soup, Northumberland lamb, pudding or cheese
Children: own menu, half portions
Best Room Rate: £40 per person
✔   Best Bargain Break: £92 per person, 2 nights - dinner, b&b
Children: free
Facilities: 2 cots and 2 high chairs; baby-listening system

20 rooms, 5 family
Open all year
♀   Ale: Ind Coope Burton, Tetley
P Own car park

BLAKENEY, NORFOLK   **Map 6**
Ⓗ BLAKENEY HOTEL, The Quay
Tel: 01263 740 797
Just off the A149 between Cromer and Wells

This fine old building, made of flint and brick, sits in a marvellous situation overlooking the harbour, which is owned by the National Trust. The rooms are spacious, many of them with lovely views, and the family rooms contain extra bunk beds.

There are excellent facilities for families, beginning with the splendid and sizeable garden, with its smooth lawns. It is beautifully maintained, safely enclosed, and has a children's play area at one end. The games room has a pool table, table tennis and darts, and there is a full-sized snooker table as well (for over-16s only). In addition there is a heated indoor swimming pool, two saunas, a jacuzzi and a fitness room.

The public rooms are comfortable and relaxing and the spacious bar area overlooks the harbour, as does the attractive restaurant.

All in all, this is a very agreeable hotel in a lovely part of the country. One of our readers described it as 'superb all round' and we agree with that summary.

Nearby: Blakeney Point is an area of outstanding natural beauty, over 1000 acres of it, and has a great wealth of bird life. There are two observation hides and a nature trail for children. Holkham Hall, the Norfolk Shire Horse Centre, Felbrigg Hall and the North Norfolk Railway, Blickling Hall and the Norfolk Wildlife Park are all within easy reach. If the area is a paradise for naturalists, so it is for golfers, with Hunstanton, Brancaster and Sheringham close by. Boat hire is easily arranged, as are horse riding and fishing.

✕ Light lunch (12.30pm to 2pm) £3-12
   Dinner (7pm to 9.30pm) £19: table d'hote menu
   Children: own menu, half portions
   Best Room Rate: £56 per person
✔ Best Bargain Break: £62 per person per night - dinner, b&b
   Children: £6 up to 16 years
   Facilities: 8 cots and 4 high chairs; baby-listening system
   60 rooms, 2 family
   Open all year
♈ Courage
🅿 Own car park

BORROWDALE, CUMBRIA   **Map 8**
Ⓗ **STAKIS LODORE HOTEL**
Tel: 017687 77285   Fax: 017687 77343
On the B5289, south of Keswick

Many of our readers have praised this hotel, a splendid place whose traditional-looking Cumbrian slate facade gives way to an interior which is modern and very comfortable. The list of facilities on offer for families would be hard to surpass – even by the grandest hotel.

There is an indoor swimming pool, a well-equipped gym and a sauna; the priceless bonus of a supervised nursery with trained nannies from 8am to 6pm each day (and where children's meals are served); a games room; an outdoor play area; and a tennis and a squash court.

The hotel actually stands in forty acres of grounds, which include the famous falls, and there are a couple of acres of lawned garden, where several thousand geraniums are planted each year.

The fine, and difficult, balance is struck here between the needs of children, and the comfort and relaxation of adults.

To quote one of our readers: 'extremely comfortable, wonderful food, and very friendly staff. It is a marvellous place to stay'.

✕   Bar snacks (12pm to 6pm) £2-7
      Dinner (7.30pm to 9.30pm) £23
      Children: own menu
      Best Room Rate: £63 per person
✔   Best Bargain Break: £51 per person per night - dinner, b&b
      Children: from £5 to £25 depending on age (includes meals)
      Facilities: 14 cots and 12 high chairs; baby-listening to every room
      75 rooms, 10 family
🅿   Own car park

BOURNEMOUTH, DORSET **Map 2**

Ⓟ THE RIVERSIDE, Tuckton Bridge

Tel: 01202 429 210

On the outskirts of Christchurch. Take the A3059 (off the A35) and head for Southbourne

The Riverside is a charming building, low-built, with bay windows and a steeply pitched roof with dormer windows; and it has a splendid position by the water at Tuckton Bridge.

Customers can take full advantage of the river views, particularly from the large terrace below the pub. Inside, there are wide windows at one end of the bar, an agreeable room with brick walls and wood panelling. The spacious restaurant also looks out to the water on one side. It is a bright and comfortable area, where smoking is prohibited. At one end there is a children's play area, with things to ride on and climb on and a ball swamp.

Food is served all day every day, and high chairs are available.

✕ (11.30am to 10pm; Sun from 12pm) £2-8: a range of hot and cold food
Children: own menu

🍷 Ale: Boddington's and guests

NR BRADFORD ON AVON, WILTS   **Map 2**
Ⓗ **WOOLLEY GRANGE**
Tel: 01225 864 705
At Woolley Green, off the B3105 north-east of Bradford-on-Avon

This 17th-century manor house is an engaging sight, built as it is from a warm-looking limestone and with its pointed gables and tall chimneys. It was a family home for several hundred years until Mr and Mrs Chapman adapted it several years back as a country house hotel. Style is the keynote from the moment you step into the wood-panelled hall with its patterned plaster ceiling and comfortable chairs and sofas.

The original decor is maintained in the sitting rooms and the attractive dining room; the Long Room, which is part library, part television room and part games room, is a delight. So are the bedrooms, which are all differently furnished and decorated but in every case reflect the owners' wishes to provide their guests with comfortable and elegant surroundings.

The huge Victorian conservatory, with its excellent cane furniture, is a lovely place to sit over coffee or something stronger. Outside, there are stretches of garden and a stone-paved terrace where you can have alfresco meals. Through a gate, you will find a heated swimming pool, a croquet lawn in an enclosed area, two grass tennis courts (by this year more all weather courts will have been added), and a badminton court. There are fourteen acres of garden in which to relax, and children can enjoy the 'Bear Garden', which has swings, a slide, a climbing frame and a small enclosed football pitch. As well as the Moulton bicycles provided at the hotel, guests can try an authentic Indian trishaw.

Amid all these comforts and excellent facilities it has been remembered that many adults have young children who also have to be cared for. This is done with a will, too. There are plenty of cots and high chairs and certain rooms are interconnecting and can form family suites.

Woolley Bear's Den occupies a large barn and is packed with Little Tikes toys and games for younger children; there is also a pool table, table tennis and table football for older children. A nanny is in attendance every day (from 10am to 6pm) and the children can be fed in the nursery off the playroom; lunch is at noon and tea at 5pm. What a boon for parents, who can enjoy their food in peace!

The hotel has a notably good chef and the same attention to detail goes into the buying of the raw ingredients for the dining room. The hotel has a two-acre kitchen garden which provides the fruit and vegetables.

This is a really splendid hotel which provides marvellous facilities, and a proper welcome, for all the family. It well deserved its 1992 'Parent Friendly' Award not to mention its Gold Award in the 1996 edition of the Guide.

Nearby: If you can tear yourself away from the comforts of Woolley Grange there is a range of places to visit. The beautiful city of Bath is very close, as are Corsham Court, Sheldon Manor, Lacock Abbey and Bowood House, which has a wonderful adventure playground. Longleat Safari Park is also within reach, with Stourhead a little further south. Riding and clay pigeon shooting can be arranged and the hotel provides bicycles and local maps to guide you. The route along the Kennet and Avon Canal is recommended.

✕ Terrace menu (12pm to 3pm and 7pm to 10pm) £4-12: chicken & vegetable stir-fry, smoked salmon, hamburger, grilled fish; Dinner (7pm to 10pm) £29: breast of guinea fowl, seared scallops with pea puree, glazed lemon tart or farmhouse cheeses Children: own menu

Best Room Rate: £50 per person
✔ Best Bargain Break: £60 per person per night - dinner, b&b
Children: free up to 2 years; £3.50 from 2 to 12; £7.50
thereafter
Facilities: 15 cots and 12 high chairs; baby-listening system;
nursery with a nanny
22 rooms, 3 suites, 3 sets interconnecting
Open all year
🅿 Own car park

BRANSFORD, WORCS   Map 4
🅟 THE FOX
Tel: 01886 832 247
On the A 4103 south-west of Worcester

This is a handsome old village inn and its outward appearance
disguises the great amount of space available inside. There are a
number of connecting rooms of different sizes and the family dining
area has a grotto-like atmosphere with its eccentric wooden beams
and pillars and its brown textured ceiling. The windows on two sides
overlook an enclosed garden, which has many bench tables with sun
umbrellas (it was July when we visited).
Wooden beams dominate overhead and the bar area has a wooden
ceiling; throughout the pub is a profusion of copper jugs and horse
brasses and other artefacts.
This is very much a family pub with plenty of high chairs, a
children's menu, baby-changing facilities, an outdoor playground
and an indoor play area, Adventure Island, which is built on the
grand scale.

✕ Food (12 to 9.30pm; until 10pm at weekends) £2-9: cajun
chicken, home-made fish & chips, steak, prawn platter
Children: own menu
♈ Ale: Greenall's, Tetley

BRIDGWATER, SOMERSET   **Map 2**
℗ QUANTOCK GATEWAY
Tel: 01278 423 593
Just west of the town centre. Follow the A35 towards Minehead

....

A part of this extensive pub is a grand old sandstone building, once called Halesleigh Towers. It now houses the family dining area, a substantial room with wood-panelled walls, on which there are a variety of prints; it is comfortably furnished with paddled settles.

Wide windows look out over the garden, which has several bench tables on the lawn and a children's play area. Children also have an indoor play area with a variety of amusements.

The main bar is a high-ceilinged room with brick walls and wood panelling and there are a number of other rooms, separated by wooden pillars and screens. It is nicely done and there is a very pleasant dining room on one side with tall windows.

As befits a family pub/restaurant many high chairs are available and it is open throughout the day.

....

✕ (11.30am to 10pm; from noon on Sundays) £2-8: a range of hot and cold food
   Children: own menu
♀ Ale: Boddington's and guests
🅿 ample

BRIGHTON, EAST SUSSEX   **Map 3**
® BROWNS RESTAURANT, 3/4 Duke Street
Tel: 01273 323 501

To the west of The Lanes. From Kings Road on the seafront, turn into Ship Street which runs into Duke Street

Brighton has its raffish side ('London by the Sea') but it is balanced by its great charm, some splendid architecture, including the extraordinary Royal Pavilion, and many tourist attractions.

For an excellent family restaurant you need look no further than Browns. We recommend all the branches of this small group (see Bath, Bristol, Cambridge, Oxford and London) and the Brighton establishment maintains the same admirable standards as the others.

It is a cheerful and bustling place, very busy when we had lunch there on an August day, and there was a good complement of families. Several high chairs are provided plus a well equipped mother and baby room. Children have their own menu, which includes a free ice cream, or can eat half portions from the main menu, on which there is always a fish dish for under a fiver. We ate the fish of the day, fillet of red bream, which was correctly cooked; moist and with an agreeable sauce.

The high-ceilinged room is decorated in the familiar Browns style. The walls are painted cream and have a number of mirrors scattered about; there are several skylights and ceiling fans; potted plants are abundant; and the wooden tables and bentwood chairs are complemented by padded benches along the walls.

Browns is a very welcoming restaurant for families and offers very good value for money. The relaxed atmosphere is due in no small degree to the cheerful and youthful staff.

You should note that Browns has a pleasant bar a couple of doors away and breakfasts are served from 8am.

✕   (11am to 11.30pm; Sun from noon) £2-11: pasta with various sauces, fisherman's pie, sirloin steak, burgers, poached salmon Children: own menu, half portions

🅿   multi-storey nearby

NR BRIGHTON, EAST SUSSEX   Map 3
Ⓟ DEVIL'S DYKE, Poynings
Tel: 01273 857 256

North of Brighton off the A23. Follow the signs for Devil's Dyke

Follow your nose right up to the top of the hill and you will be rewarded by fantastic views over miles of Sussex countryside; and there is the bonus of being able to watch the hang-gliders launch themselves, foolhardy souls, into space.

This family pub and restaurant is an extremely popular spot – especially at weekends. It's a huge place, with windows on all sides to take advantage of the wonderful views. It's cheerful and bustling, with Laura Ashley wallpaper, wooden pillars, padded benches, lots of prints on the walls, alcoves here and there to induce a feeling of intimacy and a long curved bar which has a selection of real ales.

The pub is firmly aimed at the family market – there are a dozen or more high chairs, a mother and baby room and an indoor play area. On a fine day you can sit on the paved terrace or the grass outside and luxuriate in the rolling expanse of countryside below you.

✕   (11.30am to 10pm) £2-8: a range of hot and cold food
      Children: own menu

♀   Ale: Boddington's and guests

🄿   Lots

BRISTOL, AVON   **Map 2**
® BROWNS RESTAURANT, 38 Queens Road
Tel: 0117 930 4777
Next to the Bristol Museum and opposite the triangle

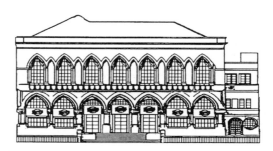

This is a more recent offspring of the excellent Browns chain (there are others in Bath, Brighton, Cambridge, London and Oxford, qv) and it is housed in a wonderful and stately building which began life as the town library and then became the Students' Union refectory. There are tables on the terraces at the front among the substantial stone pillars and inside you will find a huge high-ceilinged room with tables set out on two different levels.

Plenty of space is left around a long wooden bar and there are alcoves here and there, one with padded benches and Lloyd Loom chairs. The main restaurant has ceiling fans, wide windows, a profusion of potted plants and nice wooden furniture. It is a lively place, with youthful and cheerful staff, and it offers an excellent range of food at reasonable prices.

Families are made very welcome and there are plenty of high chairs, a children's menu and a well-equipped mother and baby room.

✗   (11am to 11.30pm; Sun from noon) £2-11: Caesar salad, pasta with various sauces, fisherman's pie, roast pork ribs, fresh vegetable bake
          Children: own menu, half portions
🅿   Meters or public car parks

BRIXHAM, DEVON   **Map 1**
Ⓗ BERRY HEAD HOTEL
Tel: 01803 853 225/858 583

This attractive house, built from mellow stone and topped by dormer windows, began life as a military hospital early in the 19th century. A couple of decades later it became the home of the Reverend Henry Francis Lyte who wrote the evocative "Abide With Me", and many other hymns, in the grounds of the house.

Just like the notable cleric, guests can enjoy the six acres of lawned gardens, framed by stately trees; and there are unrivalled views of the sea (especially across Tor Bay) and the coastline. Next door is Berry Head Country Park, now owned by the National Trust.

You can linger over the same views from the various public rooms: from the wood-panelled lounges with their comfortable chairs and sofas; and from the spacious bar next door. Outside there is an extensive terrace, a delightful spot to loiter in the sunshine with a drink or a meal.

The facilities at the Berry Head include an indoor heated swimming pool (and there is an outdoor salt water pool a short distance from the hotel), a spa bath, a croquet lawn, and, an unusual feature, a petanque court.

Nearby: the busy fishing port of Brixham is a short walk from the hotel and, as well as the Berry Head Country Park, you can take a stroll along the adjacent coastal path - all the way to Kingswear if you are feeling fit. There are many other attractions within easy reach including the Dart Valley Railway, Dawlish Warren, Compton Castle, Buckfast Abbey and the Torbay Aircraft Museum.

....

✕   Bar snacks (12 to 2pm & 7pm to 9pm) £2-12: seafood salad, beef & ale pie, smoked haddock & mushroom crumble, sirloin steak;
Dinner (7pm to 9.30pm) £18: prawn & brie in pastry, braised lamb shanks, pudding and cheese
Children: own menu, half portions
Best Room Rate: £35 per person
Best Bargain Break: £99 to £140 per person, 3 nights - dinner,

b&b
Children: under 5 free; 5 to 14 years £10, b&b
Facilities: cots, high chairs and baby listening
35 rooms, 1 family
Open all year
♀ Ale: Dartmoor, Marston's, Tetley
P ample

BROCKENHURST, HANTS   Map 3
Ⓗ WATERSPLASH HOTEL, The Rise
Tel: 01590 622 344
On the B3055

This hotel is situated in a quiet road, and the various extensions do not hide the original Victorian high roofs and dormer windows. The elegant dining room overlooks the garden, as does the welcoming lounge bar; another comfortable lounge, with a bay window, is nearby.

The family bedrooms (usually with a double and two single beds) are at the top of the house and have the benefit of plenty of space. With their sloping ceilings and wide dormer windows, they are light and bright and furnished in an appealing style.

The large gardens are sheltered by mature trees and are beautifully kept. The sizeable heated outdoor swimming pool has a terrace with picnic tables and is located by the kitchen garden, which supplies fresh fruit and vegetables for the hotel, and there is a children's play area. Other facilities include a games room with a snooker table; and a cards and board games area can be used by guests. The Watersplash is an excellent family hotel in a most attractive area of the country.

Nearby: This is the heart of the New Forest, with beautiful country-side and pleasant villages all around; a lovely place to walk and browse. There are many places to visit within easy reach: the famous motor museum and stately home at Beaulieu, the Bucklers Hard Maritime Museum, the New Forest Butterfly Farm, the Bolderwood Arboretum

with its delightful walks, Paultons Park which offers splendid entertainment for families, and Broadlands, the home of Palmerston and
later of Lord Mountbatten. In addition, there are some excellent sandy
beaches less than half an hour's drive away.

....

✗   Bar snacks (12pm to 2pm) £2-5: scampi & chips, fried chicken
      & chips, ploughman's, filled baked potatoes;
      Dinner (7.30pm to 8.30pm) £18: garlic mussels, pot roast
      venison, pudding and cheese
      Children: high teas, half portions
      Best Room Rate: £35 per person
✔   Best Bargain Break: £90 per person, 2 nights - dinner, b&b
      Children: cots free; one third of adult rate from 4 to 10 years;
      half the adult rate from 10 to 16 years
      Facilities: 3 cots and 3 high chairs; baby-listening to all rooms
      24 rooms, 6 family
      Open all year
P   Own car park

BURNLEY, LANCASHIRE   **Map 8**
Ⓟ THE FIGHTING COCKS
Tel: 01282 455 069
At Cliviger, just over two miles south of Burnley football ground.

There are terrific views of the encircling countryside from this imposing stone pub, which has been converted to cater for the family market. An inn has been on the site since the 18th century and the present one was built by Grimshaw's Brewery in 1901.

The high ceilings are criss-crossed with wooden beams which in their turn are held in place by wooden pillars. Gilt mirrors sit above the padded benches and there is plenty of space to enjoy.

A room near the entrance houses a pool table and at the other end of the pub you will find the Old Barn, an inviting room with a lofty ceiling and stone walls. Beyond is a terrace with splendid views.

Families are well looked after with lots of high chairs, a children's menu, baby-changing facilities, an outdoor playground and a well-equipped indoor play area (Adventure Island).

✕   Food (served all day, every day) £2-9: home-made fish & chips, cajun chicken, prawn platter, steak
       Children: own menu

♈   Ale: Boddington's, Tetley

CAMBRIDGE, CAMBS

® BROWNS, 23 Trumpington Street
Tel: 01223 461 655
In the town centre

Map 6

Part of a small chain of restaurants (see the entries for Bath, Bristol, Oxford, London and Brighton), this is a huge building opposite the Fitzwilliam Museum. We were told that it was once the casualty department of the old Addenbrookes Hospital. It has the familiar and effective decor of cream walls, bentwood chairs, overhead fans, Edwardian mirrors and converted gas lights. It is a cheerful place which offers an excellent range of food to suit most palates, including young ones. If you need to change a baby there is a mother and baby room with good facilities and there are plenty of high chairs.

We should warn you that parking is as difficult in Cambridge as it is in Oxford. So it is best to park your car in a public car park and enjoy the sights on foot.

✗   (11am to 11.30pm; Sun from noon) £2-11: steak & mushroom & Guinness pie, toasted olive bread with sun-dried tomatoes, pasta with various sauces, roast pork ribs, fisherman's pie
Children: own menu, half portions

🅿   Meters and own car park

CAMBRIDGE, CAMBS   **Map 6**
® HOBBS PAVILION RESTAURANT, Park Terrace
Tel: 01223 367 480
On Parker's Piece, and alongside the University Arms Hotel

....

The restaurant is housed in a brick pavilion which was opened by Jack Hobbs himself in 1930 and faces Parker's Piece where the maestro learned his cricket. Its origins are clearly apparent inside and, under its high ceiling the restaurant is attractively furnished with pine tables, a dresser and old advertising signs (Wills's Gold Flake, Kops Crisps, Sunlight Soap, etc).

The back room is just as appealing and especially so to cricket lovers, with its photographs of pre-war cricketers, cigarette cards of cricketers and portraits of Ranjit Sinjhi and of Hobbs, whose career is encapsulated on a wooden plaque.

Amid such sporting nostalgia one must remember that this is a restaurant. You can eat a very full range of pancakes – savoury and sweet – and a number of char-grilled dishes.

There is a small terrace outside with a few tables, and children have the whole of Parker's Piece on which to romp.

....

✕   (Tues to Sat 12pm to 2.15pm and 6pm to 9.45pm; £3-13: pancakes, whole Dover sole, venison sausages, sirloin steak
       Children: own menu, half portions
       Closed last two weeks of August, Christmas and Easter, Sun and Mon
       No credit cards accepted

🅿   Not easy, mostly street parking

CAWSAND, CORNWALL   **Map 1**
⊕ WRINGFORD DOWN
Tel: 01752 822 287

From the B3247 south of Torpoint, follow the signs for Cawsand. The hotel's brochure gives detailed directions.

....

Wringford Down is a rare hotel for Britain in that its owners, Harvey and Andrea Jay, provide only for families; even rarer, their hotel best suits families with children up to about six years of age. Needless to say, there are plenty of cots and high chairs and an efficient baby-listening service. The children all sit down to high tea at 5 o'clock (their meals are pre-ordered at breakfast). It was a remarkable sight to see nearly thirty young children, aged from one to five, with their parents in attendance, all seated at one long table and tucking into their nosh.

This unusual hotel is housed in a nice old stone house, the main part of which is 18th century, and has been extended over the years. The facilities include a small bar, a pool table in an adjoining room, and a restaurant. There is a spacious lounge, which has a TV and a video, and a playroom alongside; there are plenty of toys and games and blackboards on which the children can scribble. A very large conservatory has been built next to the dining room, a pleasant place to snatch some moments of relaxation with a drink or a book.

The enterprising owners provide loads of amusements both indoors and out for children. There is a huge play barn which would keep the children amused for days. It has a ball pool, a huge and very practical padded playpen, a sandpit, a trampoline and climbing ropes on a special safety surface, ride-on toys, table tennis and roller skates.

Move outdoors and you can enjoy a large garden with lovely views over the surrounding countryside with a church spire on the horizon. There is a children's play area plus chickens, goats, pigs, rabbits and sheep in a walk-in enclosure. The hotel has three miniature Shetland ponies and pony rides are organised. Donkey rides are also organized.

The indoor heated swimming pool is very popular and there is also a hard tennis court.

On a practical level, a refrigerator is provided for guests, plus a microwave oven, bottle sterilizers, etc. A great boon for parents is a nursery for under 5s, run by trained nursery nurses. Older children (from 5 to 10) have a holiday club.

This hotel has excellent facilities for young families and if you fancy a gregarious holiday during which you can muck in with lots of other parents with young children in a 'family-friendly' atmosphere, you should visit Wringford Down.

✗   Dinner (6.30pm to 9pm): wide choice of dishes, always with a vegetarian option
      Children: high teas, small portions
      Best Room Rate: £25 per person

✔   Bargain Breaks: £75 per person, 3 nights – dinner, b and b
      Children: free up to 5 years; half price from 5 to 10
      Facilities: 12 cots and 12 high chairs; baby-listening system to every room
      12 rooms, all family, 8 sets interconnecting
      Open all year except Chrisrmas

🅿   Own car park

CHAPEL AMBLE, nr WADEBRIDGE, CORNWALL   Map 1
Ⓢ THE OLDE HOUSE
Tel: 01208 813 219, Fax: 01208 815 689
Email: theoldehouse@eclipse.co.uk
The village is off the B3314 north of Wadebridge and The Olde House is close to the village pub, the Maltsters Arms

There are thirty-seven cottages to choose from at this enterprising holiday centre and farm. It all began in 1978 when Andrew and Janice Hawkey converted a couple of old farm buildings and the venture has grown every year. The latest additions were five new cottages, finished in 1993, but made of Cornish stone and with slate roofs.

The other buildings are all built from the old stone outbuildings and every effort has been made to insert all the comforts which families on holiday require while retaining the character of the buildings. The cottages accomodate from two to eight people.

The cottages have been made from a barn, a mill, a stable and a cow house and grain store, but they have one thing in common: they have all been converted with style and good taste, and are well furnished and well equipped.

One of the great advantages of staying here is the presence of an excellent, purpose built, leisure centre. Under its vaulted roof, it has a sizeable swimming pool, a children's pool, jacuzzi, sauna and solarium. It has its own lounge area with a snooker table. Outside there is a splendid adventure playground, swings and a climbing frame, a fort, Wendy house, an old tractor, a pets corner, an information room and a new indoor adventure play area. There are also two all-weather tennis courts. A farm trail has been laid out, a pleasant walk of between one and two hours.

The Olde House is at the centre of a working farm of 500 acres and the guests are welcome to join in: and the farm animals are particularly appealing to the children. This is a marvellous place for a family holiday.

Nearby: There is no shortage of safe and sandy beaches in the area, and Daymer and Polzeath offer surfing and swimming, while Rock has sailing, wind surfing and water skiing. You can follow the coastal footpath and there are plenty of stables from which to go riding. Fishermen and golfers are well catered for. If you like to see the sights you can head for Pencarrow House, Lanhydrock House, Dobwalls Theme Park, Trerice and the Lappa Valley Railway. The children will enjoy a visit to Newquay Zoo and the Tropical Bird Gardens at Padstow.

Units: 37
Rent: £275 to £1095 a week
Other costs: linen at £3.50 a person, electricity is on a meter
Heating: central heating
As many cots and high chairs as required
Open all year

NR CHELMSFORD, ESSEX   Map 6
Ⓟ SEABRIGHT'S BARN
Tel: 01245 478 033

From the A12 going east take the B1007 northwards and then turn right at the Eagle pub. Keep going and the pub is on your right.

We don't know who Seabright was but this pub is certainly housed in an old barn conversion - and a huge one at that. Its facade is clad in black timber and the main part of the interior is a bar designed on the grandest of scales. A small forest must have been decimated in order to acquire the wood needed to make the vast cross-beams which support the towering roof, and all the pillars and other wooden supports. It's all rather splendid and there is a raised sitting area at one end - watch your head on the low beams as you seek a table.

Down below to one side there are two dining rooms under sloping roofs; wood and glass screens are used to good effect, as are the displays of old bottles and a fulsome array of prints on the walls.

Gardens are provided on both sides of the pub; a large lawned one towards which the adults will probably head, and on the other side a family affair - a terrace with plenty of bench tables and a well-equipped playground with a safe bark surface.

The family dining area is sizeable and has lots of high chairs available, as well as a baby changing room. There is a children's menu and, when we visited, part of the restaurant was laid up for a children's party. The area is cheerfully decorated and Adventure Island is located just off it, a grand indoor playroom with all the activities children enjoy.

✗ Food (12 to 9.30pm; until 10pm on Friday and Saturday) £2-9: home-made fish & chips, steak, cajun chicken, prawn platter
Children: own menu
♀ Ale: Boddington's, Tetley

NR CHESTER, CHESHIRE   Map 8
℗ THE WHEATSHEAF
Tel: 01928 722 986
From junction 14 of the M56 follow the A56 towards Chester - the pub is in the village of Dunham Hill, near Helsby

A few miles from the fine and historic city of Chester, this charming inn has a facade which is smartly painted white and enlivened by hanging baskets of flowers. To one side is a pleasant garden with a children's play area and a lovely willow tree provides some shade.

Inside, the no smoking family dining area has a beamed ceiling and a number of wooden screens. It's an agreeable room, which is complemented by an adults only dining room in a similar style: wooden panelling on the walls, padded settles and bright decorations.

There is a second substantial family dining room under a tall skylight and this leads to a patio and to Adventure Island, an indoor play area with enough equipment to keep the most demanding infant happy for several hours. High chairs are available in quantity and there are baby-changing facilities.

✗ Food (12 to 9.30pm, Sunday to Thursday; until 10pm at weekends) £2-9: home-made fish & chips, cajun chicken,

prawn platter, steak
Children: own menu
Y   Ale: Greenall's, Tetley

NR CHESTERFIELD, DERBYSHIRE   Map 7
℗ **HIGHWAYMAN, Baslow Road, Eastmoor**
Tel: 01246 566 330
On the A619 west of Chesterfield

Up on the moors, four miles outside Chesterfield, this large pub is a
useful stopping-off point for families heading for Chatsworth House,
particularly since the pub is open throughout the day.

Great care has been taken to provide the facilities which any family
would welcome. The family room itself is on two levels and has plenty
of comfortable seating. There are plenty of high chairs, a baby-changing facility, a little indoor play area with toys and Lego sets, a spacious
Fun Factory with a ball pool and all sorts of diversions for the children.

There is a sizeable garden at the back of the pub which overlooks
lovely countryside. Partly paved and partly lawned, the garden has a
children's play area and a barbecue. An extra facility during the summer months is a bouncy castle. There is another lawned area at the
front of the pub where you can sit and have a drink and a meal.

The spacious interior can cope with large numbers of families and
is an agreeable place with its comfortable furniture, wood and stained-
glass screens, pot plants and coloured lights.

The stone pub dates back to 1620 and is mentioned as the New Inn
in a Sherlock Holmes mystery. It has unrivalled views of some beautiful countryside through large picture windows.

✗   (11.30am to 10pm; Sun from 12pm) £2-8: a range of hot and
     cold food
     Children: own menu, half portions
Y   Ale: Boddington's and guests
🅿   Own car park

36

COLATON RALEIGH, nr SIDMOUTH, DEVON　　　**Map 1**
Ⓢ **DRUPE FARM**
Tel: 01395 568 838 Fax: 01395 567 882
Website: www.drupefarm.co.uk
On the B3178 west of Sidmouth.

The conversion of old farm buildings (some dating back to the 17th
century) was carried out in the late seventies with great success. The
smart cottages, some built from the local pink-tinged stone and others
painted white, form a natural courtyard around a lawned garden with
lots of cheerful flowers and shrubs.

Drupe Farm is just off the main street of the attractive village and
the shops and a smart-looking pub (The Otter) are within a short stroll.

Most of the fifteen properties sleep up to four people, while two
can sleep six and two others can sleep up to seven people. There are
plenty of high chairs and cots available. The properties have plenty of
space and are comfortably furnished and smartly decorated, since a
major programme of refurbishment was completed a few years ago.
We looked at several cottages including Hayes Wood, one of the
largest; it is a very bright house which can accommodate seven people.
Tidwell Cottage has a splendid semi-circular living room with a wall
of five windows which overlook the gardens; a vast wooden beam runs
across the ceiling. We were most impressed by Drupe Farm, a lovely

spot with welcoming and comfortable cottages.

The facilities here are excellent and include a laundry, a very well-equipped games room with table tennis, a pool table, a dart board and some amusement machines; and a very safe and well-kept play area with swings, a seesaw, wooden climbing frames, a sandpit, a Wendy house, a table tennis table, and an old tractor on which children can play. There are bench tables here and a barbecue; it's a lovely spot to have an alfresco meal while the children amuse themselves.

A new and splendid addition to the fun is a barn converted to provide badminton, volleyball, a skittle alley, plus a sandpit for toddlers. There is also a new barbeque with covered seating.

Nearby: East Devon is a beautiful part of the country and Drupe Farm sits in an area of outstanding natural beauty. The countryside offers much to walkers, or you can enjoy it all from horseback. Fishermen have a good choice of river or sea fishing. There are many beaches including Budleigh Salterton, Sidmouth and Branscombe with attendant water sports. There are plenty of interesting places to see: Bicton Park, the donkey sanctuary near Sidmouth, the Farway Park, the Maritime Museum in Exeter, Killerton House, Powderham Castle and the nature reserve at Dawlish Warren.

....

Units: 12 cottages, 3 apartments
Rent: £152 to £560 a week (short breaks also available in winter)
Other costs: none
Heating: gas central heating
9 cots and 6 high chairs (stairgates also provided)
Open all year

COMPTON, nr TORQUAY, DEVON   **Map 1**
Ⓢ COMPTON POOL COTTAGES
Tel: 01803 872 241.

Off the A381 north of Totnes. The brochure has clear directions.

....

This cluster of 18th-century farm buildings was converted some years ago to provide self-catering accommodation and has been upgraded and extended in excellent style. The attractive pink-washed cottages form a courtyard which is partly lawned and has a little pond.

The nine units can accommodate from four to eight people and there is also a caravan in the paddock which can sleep four people. Many of the original features have been retained; the inglenook fireplace and stone walls of the Old Farm Cottage, for example, and the low ceilings of the Hayloft. The Cider House was constructed from half the original farmhouse and can sleep up to eight people. The Owl Loft is an interesting unit, all on one level above the games barn (the insulation is very sound). Rose Cottage is detached from the other homes and is suitable for four people.

Compton Pool is in an idyllic location, set in twelve acres with delightful gardens and ringed by gentle hills. The facilities are excellent and there is an unfussy air to the whole place; for example, toys and a variety of bikes are left in the gardens for the guests and a football net is set up on one of the lawns.

The indoor heated swimming pool (10 x 5 metres) is a great bonus and there is also a hard tennis court. The play area alongside has swings, climbing frames, a sandpit, an old tractor and a trampoline. Beyond there are five lakes, some of which are generously stocked with trout (and with coarse fish) - it's not difficult to land one for your lunch. There are lovely walks around those lakes (and in the encircling countryside) and lots of wildlife to observe.

The children can make friends with the ducks and the animals which have their homes in the orchard: chickens, rabbits, goats and Vietnamese pot-bellied pigs. There is a pony in one of the fields, which children are allowed to ride . The games barn is another great attraction; it has table football, a pool table and table tennis. On a practical note there is a laundry and a telephone.

We were very taken with Compton Pool. The care which has been

39

expended in providing accommodation of high quality was apparent. The other facilities are first class and above all we liked the relaxed atmosphere which is generated by the owners (who live on site).

Our views were endorsed by a recent visitor who wrote to tell us of 'the absolutely brilliant cottages, facilities and hosts ... great local outings ... I can't recommend highly enough'.

Nearby: Country pursuits are readily available - riding and pony trekking, walking and fishing – as are water sports, either on the River Dart or on the sea. The impressive 14th-century Compton Castle is not far, and you can visit Buckfast Abbey, the Dart Valley Railway, Powderham Castle and the Dawlish Warren Nature Reserve. The attractions of Torquay are close and there are many good sandy beaches.

Units: 9
Rent: £195 to £787 a week
Other costs: electricity on meters
Heating: electric and oil-fired central heating (free from November to April)
Cots and high chairs for each cottage
Open all year

CRANTOCK, NEWQUAY, CORNWALL   **Map 1**
Ⓗ **CRANTOCK BAY HOTEL**
Tel: 01637 830 229
Off the A3075 south of Newquay

The hotel is along the road from Crantock at West Pentire and has one of the best coastal positions we have seen. Its long grassy gardens, complete with hedges forming wind breaks and suntraps, slope down towards the sea and afford you a magnificent view of the lovely Crantock Bay – a good place to swim and loll, but you must be careful at low tide (obey the signs). It is patrolled by lifeguards during the summer; and is a great spot for surfers too.

The hotel is very much geared up to family holidays, with plenty of facilities to keep young and older occupied. The children have an activity area with a very substantial wooden fort, swings and climbing trees; there is a hard tennis court, and croquet and putting on the lawns.

The excellent indoor swimming pool (plus paddling pool for young children) is enclosed by a curved glass roof, and outside there is a sun terrace. The exercise room has some serious equipment, including a static bicycle, jogging machine and multi-gym, and you can recover on the sun terrace, in the sauna or in the spa bath.

In the field alongside the hotel there are donkeys, pigs and chickens which belong to the hotel, and it is pleasing to report that the owners grow a lot of their own vegetables (as well as providing their own free-range eggs). Children are encouraged to eat smaller versions of the adults' food – mini-dinners are served at 5pm.

Most of the rooms have fine views of the bay and beach, and some of the ground-floor rooms lead directly out to the gardens.

This is a delightful place and the prices charged are very reasonable indeed; the hotel represents outstanding value for families on holiday.

Nearby: As well as Crantock Bay, there are many good beaches for swimmers, surfers and deckchair huggers. There are many attractions around Newquay including the zoo, the Lappa Valley Railway, Dairyland Farm Park, St Agnes Leisure Park and the beautiful Elizabethan house of Trerice.

✗   Lunch (12pm to 2pm) £1-3: soup, cold buffet;
        Dinner (7pm to 8.30pm) £16: trout pate, soup, roast loin of pork,
        pudding or cheese
        Children: own menu, half portions
        Best Room Rate: £38 per person
✔   Best Bargain Break: £53 per person per night - dinner, b&b
        Children: free up to 2 years; one third of adult rate from 2-5
        years; half from 6-8 years; three-quarters from 9-12 years
        Facilities: many cots and high chairs; baby-listening
        34 rooms, 3 family
        Closed Dec and Jan
🅿   Own car park

CREWE, CHESHIRE   Map 8
Ⓟ **THE MERLIN**
Tel: 01270 213 775
On the B5076 on the outskirts of Crewe

This is a relatively new pub on the fringes of the town and the brick and glass facade gives way to a traditional interior. The great amount of space has sensibly been broken up into a number of rooms and alcoves and the predominant impression is of wood: beams, pillars, dressers and chests, and panelling. Prints decorate the walls and brassware and old bottles sit on the shelves; some of the alcoves are lined with books. It's a congenial atmosphere for everyone.

Families are very much to the fore here with their own dining area, complete with several high chairs and there is of course a children's menu. The youngsters have an outdoor play area and one indoors, the well-equipped Adventure Island. At the rear of the pub you will find a patio with bench tables.

✗   Food (12 to 9.30pm, Sunday to Thursday; until 10pm

otherwise) £2-9: prawn platter, cajun chicken, steak, home-made fish & chips

Children: own menu

♀ Ale: Bass, Boddington's, Greenall's

DAWLISH, DEVON **Map 1**
Ⓗ **RADFORDS COUNTRY HOTEL, Lower Dawlish Water**
Tel: 01626 863 322
In the countryside near Dawlish – the hotel provides an excellent map

This hotel, at the heart of which is an attractive, pink-washed thatched building, has been in the *Family Welcome Guide* since the first edition and we have had nothing but good reports of it ever since. It is everything a family hotel should be and is aimed solely at parents with young children. Many of our readers have been fulsome in their praise.

Every room is a family room and there are masses of cots and high chairs available. The owners are punctilious about the way in which their guests are cared for: the indoor pool, for example, with its separate children's pool, is always attended by a lifeguard.

Similarly, staff are on duty as baby-sitters every night from 7pm to 11.30pm and the children are monitored all the time.

The facilities are comprehensive: a games room with a pool table, skittles, darts, table tennis, space invaders, etc; a play area with swings, a slide, a large wooden fort, a cableway and an adventure course, a roundabout and a climbing frame; a play room (open from 9am to 8pm) with a selection of toys and a ball pool; an outdoor badminton court; and, of course, the indoor pool. Entertainments for the children are organized almost every day, including a playgroup three mornings a week, and they have a chance to learn horse riding.

Nearby: There are many sandy beaches close by, including Dawlish Warren, which has a nature reserve adjoining it, where a huge variety of birds can be seen. Nature lovers will also be interested in the Parke Rare Breeds Farm, while the Dartmoor Wildlife Park is a bit further away. Other nearby attractions include Powderham Castle, Bicton Park, the remarkable cottage of A la Ronde and the busy resort of Torquay.

....

✗   Dinner (6pm to 7pm): trout mousse, carbonade of beef, strawberry romanoff
           Children: own menu, half portions
           Best Room Rate: £46 (full board) per person
✔   Best Bargain Break: £120 per person, 3 nights - dinner, b&b
           Children: from no charge to two-thirds the adult cost, depending on season
           Facilities: numerous cots and high chairs; baby-listening system to each room and baby patrol from 7pm to 11.30pm
           37 rooms, all family, 11 sets interconnecting
           Closed mid-Nov to Mar (open Christmas and New Year, and in Feb at half term)
♀   Ale: Courage
🅿   Own car park

DAWLISH WARREN, DEVON   **Map 1**
Ⓗ **LANGSTONE CLIFF HOTEL**
Tel: 01626 868 000   Fax: 01626 868 006
Website: www.langstone-hotel.co.uk
Take the signs for Dawlish Warren off the A379.

....

This is a large and well-organized hotel in a delightful setting amid twenty acres of expansive lawns and woodland. Most of the rooms have balconies which overlook the gardens and the sea beyond. It is a peaceful spot and we were lucky enough to visit on a hot summer's day when the guests were lolling in the gardens.

The public rooms are spacious and appealing, and the long terrace is a good spot on which to enjoy a drink. The facilities are plentiful, with an outdoor and an indoor swimming pool, both with paddling pools, a hard tennis court and a play area for children in the nineteen acres of gardens; and there is now an indoor play area. You can also play snooker, table tennis, carpet bowls or darts, and there is a golf course within half a mile with concessionary rates for guests. Sandy beaches lie no more than 500 yards from the hotel.

With plenty of high chairs and cots available and forty family rooms (including family suites with two bedrooms), the hotel is firmly in the family market and copes with its demands with great succcss.

Nearby: Right next door there is the Dawlish Warren Nature Reserve, with plenty of Brent geese and other wildfowl. Other attractions within reach are Powderham Castle, Castle Drogo, Parke Rare Breeds Farm, Compton Castle, the Dart Valley Railway and Buckfast Abbey. There are many excellent beaches on which to loll, starting with Dawlish Warren, from which dogs are banned, and those around Torquay.

....

✗ Coffee shop (10am to 7pm) £2-5: soup, cottage pie, roast of the day, beef curry & rice, plaice & chips;
Dinner (7pm to 9pm) £15: Brixham crab, navarin of lamb, pudding and cheese
Children: high teas, half portions
Best Room Rate: £41 per person

✔ Best Bargain Break: £90-£120 per person, 2 nights - dinner, b&b
Children: free up to 10 years; half price thereafter
Facilities: 20 cots and 20 high chairs; baby-listening system to every room
67 rooms, 40 family
Open all year

Ⴟ Ale: John Smith

🅿 Own car park

NR DERBY, DERBYSHIRE   **Map 7**
Ⓟ BARTLEWOOD LODGE, Dale Road, Ockbrook
Tel: 01332 677 198
On the A6096 near the village of Ockbrook

Located in a most attractive spot in the countryside high above the outskirts of Derby, this is an appealing low-pitched building, surrounded by garden lawns with plenty of bench tables.

The spacious open-plan interior spreads out from a central bar area. It is a comfortable pub with a cheerful decor, where plenty of wood – beams and panelling – is in evidence. The L-shaped conservatory is a pleasant place to sit, whatever the weather.

The facilities for families are outstanding. Plenty of high chairs are available and there is a mother and baby room; in addition, the Charlie Chalk Fun Factory will keep young children amused for hours with its collection of toys and playthings which include a ball swamp, a slide and cartoons. Alongside there is a pets' corner with goats, rabbits, guinea pigs and ducks, and the outdoor play area is very well equipped.

The pub is open all day and food is available most of the time.

✗   (11.30am to 10pm; Sun from 12pm) £2-8: a range of hot and cold food
      Children: own menu
♀   Ale: Boddington's and guests
🅿   Own car park

NR DUNSTER, SOMERSET   Map 2
Ⓢ **DUDDINGS COUNTRY HOLIDAYS, Timberscombe**
Tel: 01643 841 123.
On the A396 on the Dunster side of the village.

....

Duddings has an enviable location alongside the valley created by the River Avill; from the cottages you have a delightful view of the gentle wooded hills and scattered fields.

The cottages have been built from the old barns, whose walls were made from the attractive local stone, which is reddish-brown in colour. The smallest properties can accommodate two people and the largest twelve, with half a dozen cottages able to sleep between four and six people. The English Tourist Board has graded the properties as 'Four Keys – Highly Commended'.

We were impressed with the care which has clearly been exercised in converting the buildings. The original features, the ancient beams and stone walls, have been retained and enhanced by the provision of comfortable and stylish furniture and excellent decorations. There are fitted carpets throughout the cottages and the kitchens have everything a cook would need, including microwave ovens. The proprietors are on the spot to ensure that the guests are well looked after.

The cottages have the great advantage of a lovely setting, and there are little picnic areas with bench tables, set amongst the trees in the immaculately maintained gardens. The cottages also have their own little patios where you can have a quiet drink or an al fresco meal.

The other facilities are excellent, too. There is loads of space for the children to play in the paddock and in the fields and alongside the river; Duddings has the bonus of a hard tennis court, an indoor heated swimming pool, which is four feet in depth and suitable for most members of a family, a putting green, pool room and a table tennis table. There are many pets with whom the children can make friends: horses, doves, ducks and peacocks. This is a marvellous spot for a family holiday in an area which has so much to offer.

Nearby: Fishermen are well catered for on the local rivers, the Exe and the Barle, and there are brown trout in the Avill, which flows through the Duddings' grounds. It is a great area for pony trekking and there are several riding centres in the vicinity. The beaches of the north Somerset coast are close and a new leisure pool has been built in Minehead. There are many attractions to see: Dunster Castle and water mill, the West Somerset Railway, Cleeve Abbey, Tropiquaria Wildlife Park, Beeworld, the Lynton and Lynmouth Cliff Railway and so on..

Units: 12
Rent: £145 to £1320 a week (off-peak breaks available - a minimum of 3 nights)
Other costs: electricity (at cost)
Heating: convector heaters in all rooms
4 cots and 4 high chairs
Open all year

EAST PORTLEMOUTH, nr SALCOMBE, DEVON　　　**Map 1**
Ⓗ⑤ **GARA ROCK HOTEL**
Tel: 01548 842 342
Website: www.gara.co.uk
Take the road to the coast from the A379 at Frogmore

The hotel was originally a row of coastguards' cottages and there are glorious views of the cliffs, the sea and the surrounding National Trust land. You can see a sandy cove down below which can be reached via a footpath. Gara Rock provides flexible family accommodation, with more than 20 suites which house four, six or eight people; some have sofa-beds and some have bunk bedrooms for children. They also have kitchens and guests can opt to cook for themselves or use the hotel restaurant and bistro. The largest unit is the balcony suite which can take nine people and has spectacular views. However, a reorganisation will enable some of the apartments to be changed into a series of en-suite bedrooms – twenty in total – and thus provide an even greater degree of flexibility.

Great care is taken here to make life as easy as possible for parents, with plenty of cots and high chairs and a baby-listening system. There is a lot for the children to do – apart from the beach, there are acres of grassy garden in which there is a heated outdoor swimming pool and paddling pool, a hard tennis court and an adventure playground with a wooden boat. The pets include rabbits and Guinea pigs. Inside is a games room with table tennis and table football, and the hotel organises various entertainments like the weekly Magic Show and children's party. A playgroup is organised for two hours a day on five days of the week for children of three years and upwards, and there is a room for teenagers, aptly called the Wreck Room.

All the family can enjoy the superb walks in this beautiful part of Devon, even though there is so much to do at the hotel that you need never leave its grounds. On a sunny summer day you can have a relaxing lunch on the lawns, and the barbecue is usually in full swing. Children's suppers are available at 6.30pm and food is available right through the day.

This hotel manages to care for families extremely well and offers outstanding value for money. All sorts of extra activities are organized: guided coastal walks, swimming galas, magic shows, children's parties, and quiz nights; and a clown is in attendance at weekends.

Nearby: If you fancy some sightseeing, there is much to choose from within easy reach. The children will enjoy the National Shire Horse Centre and the Dartmoor Wildlife Centre; enthusiasts will head for the Dart Valley Railway; while the Dartington Cider Press Centre has an array of craft shops and a couple of restaurants. Buckfast Abbey, the Torbay Aircraft Museum, and Compton Castle are all nearby, as is the busy resort of Torquay.

....

Units: 26 suites
Rent: £78 to £176 for 3 nights; £215 to £1099 per week
Other costs: none
Heating: central heating
Facilities: 20 cots and 15 high chairs
Open February to November

EVESHAM, WORCESTERSHIRE   Map 4
⊕ EVESHAM HOTEL, Coopers Lane
Tel: 01386 765 566 (Freephone reservations: 0800 716 969)
Just off the A44 by the river, and close to the town centre

The building was modernized early in the 19th century but its origins lie back in the 16th century. A modern wing was added behind the original building a few years ago and as you approach the entrance it is difficult to believe that there are 39 bedrooms here. We looked at several of them and were most impressed by the amount of space which is provided and at the high degree of comfort. Not only are the decorations and the furniture of a high quality but it is indicative of the concern for guests' comfort that easy chairs are provided in each room. There is ample space, too, for a cot or an extra bed.

In the original building we looked at a marvellous family suite under the rafters. As you enter, the children's bedroom has two single beds and bean bags as seats; down a few stairs there is a sitting room under a high ceiling and up above is a double bedroom. It is a delightful set of rooms and has a large bathroom with Victorian style fittings.

Many of the bedrooms look out to the gardens, over two acres of lawns with bright flowers and many mature trees, including several ancient mulberry trees and a venerable cedar. You can laze around on the terrace or try your hand at croquet or putting, and there is play equipment for children, including a slide, a swing, a climbing frame and a trampoline. If the weather is unkind there is an indoor play area with toys, a slide and many board games. Above all, you can take some exercise in the indoor swimming pool, where the provision of toys, floating mats and water pistols ensures plenty of fun; table tennis and table football are also provided.

Great care is taken at this hotel to welcome guests of any age; families are cared for in the same way as everyone else. Parents are given a baby box in case they've forgotten anything. There is a vast range of drinks to sample in the bar. It is an extremely comfortable and friendly place; any hotelier who leaves copies of the Dandy and Beano in the lavatories gets our vote every time.

Nearby: Beautiful countryside and all the interesting places in the Cotswolds lie close to hand: Sudeley Castle, Cotswold Farm Park, Sezincote, Snowshill Manor, Cotswold Wildlife Park, Ragley Hall and Coughton Court. The famous towns and villages are within easy reach: Stratford-upon-Avon, Broadway, Stow-on-the-Wold, Winchcombe, Bourton-on-the-Water and Chipping Campden.

✗ Lunch (12.30pm to 2pm) £19: crab cocotte, Hereford pork, pudding or cheese (or a buffet lunch for around £7);
Dinner (7pm to 9.30pm) £21: watercress mousse, roast rack of lamb, sticky toffee pudding
Children: own menu, half portions
Best Room Rate: £48 per person

✔ Best Bargain Break: £53 per person per night - dinner, b&b
Children: £3 for each year (ie £3 for a one-year-old, £6 for a two-year-old, etc)
Facilities: 4 cots and 4 high chairs; baby-listening system
39 rooms, 2 family suites

P Own car park

FALMOUTH, CORNWALL   **Map 1**
Ⓗ **ROYAL DUCHY HOTEL, Cliff Road**
Tel: 01326 313 042
Near the town centre and overlooking the bay

The hotel, which celebrated its centenary in 1993, is the resort's only four-star hotel and has a superb situation overlooking the broad sweep of Falmouth Bay. Recently renovated, it is in pristine order with very appealing public rooms. The spacious L-shaped bar looks over the terrace and the gardens and has the great bonus of views out to sea, as does the elegant dining room.

We looked at several family bedrooms and were impressed by the amount of space provided and the first class facilities which you would expect of such an hotel. Many of the rooms have panoramic views over the bay. The well-designed leisure centre (for the use only of guests) has a sizeable pool, a paddling pool and a sauna, solarium and spa bath; alongside there is a games room with table tennis, snooker and amusement machines.

Food is one of the great pleasures of a holiday and the hotel has earned two AA rosettes for its cuisine. In addition, the hotel has an all-year-round programme of musical entertainment.

Nearby: Leisure facilities available locally and include golf, tennis, squash, fishing, horse riding and every type of water sport. Many safe, sandy, beaches are within easy reach. Other attractions include Trelissick Garden, Pendennis Castle, the Seal Sanctuary, Goonhilly Earth Station, Flambards Theme Park, Godolphin House and St Michael's Mount.

✕   Bar snacks (12pm to 2pm) £3-8: wild mushroom pithivier, charcutier tortellini, fried Cornish cod, chicken and apricot pie; Lunch (12.30pm to 2pm) £10: chicken and pistachio terrine, braised beef olive, pudding;
Dinner (7pm to 9pm) £20: crabmeat and pink grapefruit salad, roast crown of lamb, pudding or cheese
Children: own menu, half portions
✔   Best Bargain Break: £74-118 per person, 2 nights - dinner, b&b

Best Room Rate: £66 per person
Children: free under 2 years; £12 from 2 to 5; £31 from 6 to 11;
£41 thereafter (including meals)
Facilities: 4 cots and 4 high chairs; baby-listening system
43 rooms, 8 family
Open all year

P Ample

FARNBOROUGH, SURREY　　　　　　　　　　　　**Map 3**
Ⓟ **MONKEY PUZZLE**
Tel: 01252 546 654
On the A327, south of Junction 4A of the M3.

....

The original brick pub has been painted light yellow and has been radically expanded to form a spacious family pub and restaurant.

The whole building is encircled by lawns and terraces (with plenty of bench tables) and there is a particularly pleasing stretch of lawn, with an array of shrubs and trees, to the rear of the pub. A play unit has been set up here for the children and, in the summer months, a bouncy castle adds to their fun.

The bar area leads to the patio. It is a congenial spot, with panelled walls, wide windows, padded settles and a large brick fireplace.

Alongside, there is a dining area in a similar style, and the family restaurant is a capacious open-plan room but divided by screens and a central fireplace into smaller units. One of these is an almost circular room, panelled entirely in wood, with a high pointed ceiling. It all hangs together very well and there is a play zone here for the smaller children. High chairs are plentiful and there is a nappy-changing facility.

....

✕　　(11.30am to 10pm) £2-8: a range of hot and cold food
　　　Children: own menu
♇　　Ale: Boddington's and guests
P　Ample

FAR SAWREY, CUMBRIA   **Map 8**
Ⓗ **THE SAWREY HOTEL**
Tel: 015394 43425
On the B5285, one mile from the west side of the Windermere car ferry

....

The hotel is situated close to the famous lake, and the ferry runs every twenty minutes during the summer and is always busy. The core of the building is of 18th century origin and various additions have been made over the years; for example, the stables were made into a bar, called the Claife Crier, and for parents who fancy a sustaining glass of Theakston's it is useful to know that there are various alcoves, away from the bar, where they and their children can settle down. There is a good range of bar snacks available here at lunchtimes.

There is another bar in the main part of the hotel and a large lounge with plenty of easy chairs. The family rooms, functional and comfortable, provide adequate space. One of the hotel's bonuses is its lovely lawned garden, partly enclosed by hedges; it's a fine place to sit in the sun.

The hotel offers excellent value to families, especially if you take advantage of their four-day or weekly terms in the off-peak periods.

Nearby: The village of Near Sawrey is famous as the home of Beatrix Potter and a pilgrimage to her house, Hill Top, will no doubt be on the programme. In the heart of the lakes, you will hardly be short of holiday diversions, even on the simplest level of walking through the lovely countryside or enjoying the available water sports. Within easy reach are the Fell Foot Park; Grizedale Forest with its Wildlife Centre and Nature Trails; the Steamboat Museum at Windermere; John Ruskin's house, Brantwood, which you can also see from the deck of the steam yacht Gondola which cruises on Coniston Water; the Lakeside and Haverthwaite Railway; and so on.

....

✕   Bar Snacks (noon to 2.30pm) £2-8: rollmop herring, Cumberland sausage, local smoked trout, sirloin steak;
Dinner (7pm to 8.45pm) £17: 5 courses changed each day (eg, Stilton vol au vents, poached salmon, fresh fruit salad, cheese
Children: own menu, half portions

Best Room Rate: £32 per person

✔ Best Bargain Break: £80 per person 2 nights - dinner, b&b (four nights off-peak is £114)

Children: cots £5; half price to age 13

Facilities: 4 cots and 2 high chairs; baby-listening to each room

18 rooms, 3 family, 1 set interconnecting

Open all year except second half of December

♀ Ale: Black Sheep, Theakston's, Jennings, John Smiths

🅿 Own car park

FOWEY, CORNWALL   **Map 1**
Ⓗ **FOWEY HALL**
Tel: 01726 833 866

....

Fowey Hall sits in an exalted position above the old port, a town of steep and twisting streets, one of whose most famous daughters was Daphne du Maurier, the author of many renowned novels including "My Cousin Rachel" and "Frenchman's Creek". The Hall was completed in 1899 for Sir Charles Hanson, a local boy who made his fortune in Canada, returned to his birthplace and spared no expense in building the house of his dreams, the symbol of his worldly success.

Fowey Hall is a recent addition to the small group of hotels run by Nigel Chapman and Nicholas Dickinson, whose philosophy is to cater for the needs of all the family. As at their hotels in Bradford on Avon, Malmesbury and Moonfleet (q.v.) they provide all the facilities which will ensure a happy visit to the hotel for everyone - from the tiniest baby to the most senior grandparent - and anyone in between. It is a difficult balancing act which they and their staff achieve with great aplomb.

The building itself is an imposing one: pillars lead you towards the entrance and there are solid towers at each corner. Within you will find many splendid rooms, some of them panelled in oak, such as the entrance hall, the library with its interesting oil-paintings and fascinating illustrations of the house as it used to be, and the spacious dining room. The drawing room has elaborate moulded ceilings and, from the public rooms, there are soothing views of the gardens and, beyond, the port, the Fowey Estuary and the English Channel.

The great advantage for families staying at Fowey Hall is the flexibility of the accommodation; there are eight pairs of interconnecting rooms and eight suites - and those suites are very large and can cope with two parents and a couple of children with ease. For example, the Hanson suite seems to have acres of space, including a sitting area in the upper part of one of the towers. It is a stately, high-ceilinged room, well-matched by its substantial antique furniture - and the huge gilt mirrors in the bathroom add to the feeling of luxury. Next door is a smaller bedroom which can be used by other members of a family.

There are ample facilities for adults and children alike: five acres of lawned gardens for a start; and you can enjoy the views from the long outdoor terrace. To one side there is a sizeable swimming pool which is covered by a high-domed conservatory. A Nintendo room is set aside for older children, who can also get together in the basement Bear Garden; it has a pool table, table football, air hockey and, of course, music. Younger children have a crèche which is supervised from 10am to 6pm, and children's lunches and high teas are laid on each day. There is a sophisticated baby listening system and it enables parents to dine secure in the knowledge that their children are being watched over - very important since the cooking is of a very high quality and should be enjoyed at one's leisure.

In summary, Fowey Hall is an exceptional family hotel, with excellent facilities in a popular holiday area.

Nearby: there are plenty of beaches within the vicinity and splendid walks along the South Cornwall Coast Path. Many attractions are a short journey away including Dobwalls Theme Park, Restormel Castle, the superb Lanhydrock House and the Charlestown Visitor Centre.

....

✗   Bar snacks (12 to 2pm & &pm to 9pm) £2-17: vegetable
    risotto, sausages & mash, local lobster, sirloin steak;
    Dinner (7.30pm to 9.30pm) £30: pigeon & chicken terrine,
    seafood with Mediterranean vegetables, poached pear with
    cherries
    Children: own menu
    Best Room Rate: £95 to £245 per room
    Children: free
    Facilities: cots, high chairs and baby listening
    25 rooms, 8 suites, 8 sets interconnecting
    Open all year

FYFIELD, nr ABINGDON, OXON   **Map 5**
Ⓟ **WHITE HART**
Tel: 01865 390 585
Off the A420, seven miles from Abingdon

....

This spendid old pub, built as a chantry house in the 15th century and owned by St John's College, Oxford, is located in a charming village. There is plenty of space inside and several rooms where a family can settle and feel thoroughly at ease. A wide choice of real ales and an enterprising array of food, virtually all of which is made in the premises from fresh ingredients, is always available. Children have their own menu, high chairs are provided and there is a table and chair in the Ladies to facilitate the changing or feeding of babies.

The bar sits to one side of what was once the hall, a fine room with a high ceiling criss-crossed by black beams; on the other side there is a cosy room with a large open fireplace. Families have a choice of four areas: the dining room which has an open fireplace and a low beamed ceiling; the barrel-vaulted cellar; a superb room upstairs with exposed ancient timbers; or the minstrels' gallery above the bar.

On a summer day you should head for the terrace at the back of the pub and the pretty sheltered garden which is ringed with shady trees. It also has a children's play area.

The White Hart is an exceptional pub which has been in every edition of the guide and won a special award in the first one. We are glad to confirm that its high standards are maintained.

....

✕   Food (12 to 2pm and 7pm to 10pm) £3-11: spinach strudel, fried scampi, steaks, chicken Strasbourg, vension casserole
     Children: own menu

♀   Ale: Boddington's, Hook Norton, Theakston's, Wadworth's and guests

🅿   Own car park

Nr GLOUCESTER, GLOS Map 4
℗ **CROSS HANDS, Brockworth**
Tel: 01452 863 441

At Brockworth, on the roundabout where the A417 crosses the A46.

This agreeable pub is built of stone, its facade partly pebble-dashed and enlivened by hanging baskets of flowers. It has been extended to encompass a very large family pub and restaurant with loads of high chairs, nappy changing facilities, a Fun Factory, and a play unit on one side of the pub (where a bouncy castle also makes an appearance during the summer).

A comfortable semicircular bar occupies one end of the pub and overlooks a lawned garden. Alongside, there is a wood-panelled restaurant with French windows on to a terrace. Beyond you will find a large area with stone walls and wide windows. The main restaurant has a high ceiling, wood-panelled walls and padded settles. It is a bright and cheerful spot and has one dining area on a dais. The family dining room comes next, where the Fun Factory is positioned. Doors lead out to the garden with its play area.

✕   (11.30am to 10pm) £2-8: a range of hot and cold food
       Children: own menu
♀   Ale: Boddington's and guests
🅿   Own car park

GREAT BILLING, NR NORTHAMPTON **Map 7**
ⓅⒽ THE QUAYS
Tel: 01604 417 400

From junction 15 of the M1, take the A508 and then follow the signs to the Billing Aquadrome.

This is a brand new pub which had only been open for a few days when we had lunch there. Conventionally built from brick, it has dark wood cladding and the Lodge alongside echoes the pleasant style. The Quays has a wonderful location by the Billing Aquadrome - most people love to look out over water and it is here in abundance.

There is plenty of space in this pub, which is laid out in an open-plan design. The various areas are cleverly differentiated; and the overall impression is light and bright, with appealing pastel colours - blue, green and primrose - on the walls. Wood has also been used to good effect, with lots of pillars and beams and some timber panelling. There is a pronounced and appropriate nautical flavour to the pub with many prints and other artefacts of seafaring subjects, and model boats placed here and there.

It is a very comfortable pub with a sizeable no smoking dining area and a similarly large family dining room, with plenty of high chairs. There is a children's menu and a baby changing room. Upstairs you will find an extensive indoor play area, Captain Coconuts, which has a spacious lounge for the adults and it overlooks the water.

On warmer days you can take advantage of the expansive terrace with its wooden decking. It spreads along the water and you can gaze out at the myriad small craft on the Aquadrome.

The Lodge has 60 rooms, of which 25 are family rooms and the prices are reasonable: £45.50 on weekdays and £39.50 at weekends.

✕ Food (12 to 9.30pm; until 10pm on Fridays and Saturdays, with table service) £2-13: mushroom & Stilton bake, oriental prawns, sizzling chicken, fillet steak, hot and cold buffet
Children: own menu

🍷 Ale: Boddington's, Tetley

HANDFORTH, LANCASHIRE   **Map 8**
Ⓟ WAGGON & HORSES
Tel: 0161 437 3626

From the A34 at Handforth follow the sign to Stanley Green, go past the retail park and keep going to the next junction - the pub is opposite.

....

This is a sprawling, red brick roadhouse which has been converted into a family pub. The very roomy interior contains facilities for everyone. The family dining area has windows onto the outdoor playground and the children can also have fun in Adventure Island, the indoor play area with its great array of equipment. High chairs are available in quantity and there is a baby changing room.

    The decor and furnishings are agreeable: wooden settles, booths, brick pillars and wooden screens. The pub also has a highly unusual feature - a bowling green, which appeared to our untutored eyes to be in immaculate condition.

....

✕   Food (12 to 9.30pm Sunday to Thursday; until 10pm otherwise) £2-9: home-made fish & chips, steak, prawn platter, cajun chicken
         Children: own menu
♀   Ale: Greenall's, Tetley

HARROGATE, NORTH YORKS   Map 9
® BETTYS CAFE TEAROOMS, 1 Parliament Street
Tel: 01423 502 746
Off the A61 near the town centre and opposite Montpelier Gardens

....

This is certainly not a place to be missed if you have children and are visiting this attractive town. It is a rare opportunity for parents of young children to relax in a stylish tearoom, where the high standards never waver. It is a bustling place with wide windows on to Montpelier Gardens, and the decor of marble-topped tables, Art Nouveau mirrors and 1920s-style prints is most appealing. There are real flowers on your table, real tea or coffee in your cup, and an excellent range of snacks, hot or cold meals, cakes and pastries. Live piano music is played during the evenings.

In addition, Bettys gives a proper welcome to families; apart from charming service and an interesting children's menu, it offers first-class facilities: changing mats, playpen, potties, bibs and beakers are all made available, plus many high chairs; and most of the restaurant is non-smoking. The kitchen will also provide baby foods.

....

✕   (9am to 9pm) £2-8: Swiss Rostis, Yorkshire rarebits, croutes aux champignons, club sandwiches, traditional afternoon teas, fresh cream cakes
Children: own menu, half portions
Open every day except Christmas and New Year

🅿   Street parking

Nr HARROGATE, NORTH YORKSHIRE   **Map 9**
Ⓟ RED LION
Tel: 01423 770 132
At South Stainley on the A61

....

If you are planning a visit to Ripley Castle, the famous ancestral home of the Ingilby family, you can also pause for some refreshment at the Red Lion, which is just north of the castle. It is a handsome old coaching inn, its walls festooned with climbing plants.

Inside there are numerous comfortable and inviting rooms, including a spacious bar area, nicely decorated with floral wallpaper. Padded settles sit below the many windows, there is a brick fireplace and the rooms are split up with booths. The family dining room (with plenty of high chairs and a children's menu) has three sizeable areas and more booths.

The delightful garden has well-tended lawns and the many mature trees provide shady patches. The terrace has plenty of bench tables and a playground for the children, who can also enjoy the indoor Adventure Island.

The Red Lion is an excellent family pub with a full complement of essential facilities.

....

✗   Food (12 to 9.30pm, Sunday to Thursday; until 10pm other days) £2-9: home-made fish & chips, cajun chicken, steak, prawn platter
      Children: own menu
Ⴏ   Ale: Greenall's, Tetley

63

HASTINGS, EAST SUSSEX   **Map 3**
Ⓗ BEAUPORT PARK HOTEL, Battle Road
Tel: 01424 851 222
On the A2100 between Battle and Hastings

....

The regular lines and warm red brick of this splendid Georgian mansion make a most appealing sight, especially when you take in the pillared main entrance and the dormer windows in the steep roof. It is a wonderful setting for this elegant hotel in its lovely parkland which includes a formal Italian garden with superb trees, and a tranquil sunken garden, partly enclosed by an old stone wall.

The smooth lawn at the front contains a putting green, and beyond there is a hard tennis court and a grass badminton court. At the back of the hotel is a giant chess board, a boule pitch and a croquet lawn. Above all, there is an outdoor heated swimming pool, surrounded by pleasant lawns on which to loll. Next door, there is a riding school and six squash courts; and golfers should be in their element since there is both a 9-hole and an 18-hole golf course, plus a golf driving range.

The Norwegian pine lodges, within the hotel grounds, are ideal for families. The restaurant has an excellent reputation and has been awarded a rosette.

....

✗   Bar snacks (noon to 9.30pm) £3-6
        Lunch (12.30pm to 2pm) £16
        Dinner (7pm to 9.30pm) £21
        Children: own menu, half portions
        Best Room Rate: £69 per person
✔   Best Bargain Break: £118 per person, 2 nights - dinner, b&b.
        The lodges cost £140 per night (2 adults and 3 children)
        Children free up to 16 years

Nr HEATHFIELD, EAST SUSSEX   Map 3
⊕ WEST STREET FARMHOUSE, Maynards Green
Tel: 01435 812 516
On the B2203 just south of Heathfield in the village of Maynards Green

This is a delightful brick farmhouse, built in an L-shape, parts of which date back to the 17th century. It is surrounded by nearly four acres of grounds, a large part of which comprise smooth lawns: a lovely spot for the children to play (there are some swings) and for the adults to relax. The views of the surrounding countryside are superb.

The two bedrooms, one with a double and the other with twin beds, are most attractive with their low-beamed ceilings and they overlook the garden. A bathroom is shared between them and they can both accommodate a cot.

Down below, there is a pleasant and cosy lounge with a television and a wood-burning stove, and the compact dining room is next door. A family could rent both bedrooms and have their own very peaceful self-contained unit.

Nearby: This is a delightful part of England, with glorious country-side all around and with the coastline from Brighton eastwards within easy reach. Nature lovers will head for Drusillas Park, the Seven Sisters Country Park and the Bentley Wildfowl Trust (there is also a motor museum here). Bateman's, where Rudyard Kipling wrote many of his books, is nearby, as is Herstmonceux Castle, Michelham Priory and the Bluebell Railway.

Dinner (7pm) £10 (by prior arrangement)
Children: half portions
Best Room Rate: £18 per person
Children: no charge up to 3 years; half price 3 to 10
Facilities: 1 cots and 1 high chair; baby-listening by arrangement
2 rooms
Open all year
Unlicensed
P   Own car park

HELTON, nr PENRITH, CUMBRIA   Map 8
Ⓗ **BECKFOOT HOUSE HOTEL**
Tel: 01931 713 241
Off thc A6 south of Penrith.

The house is actually about a mile south of the village of Helton, which has a pub and is itself six miles or so from Penrith. It is quite a stately house, built of stone in the late l9th century, with a large and immaculate lawn at the front with a charming sundial and a great fir tree. It is surrounded by a variety of fine trees and at the back of the house the ground slopes up to a small paddock which is aJso encircled by trees. There is plenty of room for children to play, and they have an adventure playground. There is easy access to the fells with many delightful walks and masses of wildlife to spot.

The rooms are beautifully proportioned and contain several fine marble and oak fireplaces; the spacious sitting room is furnished with a variety of comfortable easy chairs. You have splendid views of the gardens and the countryside beyond, and an open fire for cooler evenings. Board games and children's toys are available. Like the lounge, the dining room has nice wood panelling and wide windows overlooking the garden.

This is very much a house where families are made welcome, and there are cots and high chairs as well as three family rooms. As you would expect of this handsome and spacious place, they are of a generous size and very well furnished and decorated: one has a double and two single beds, and the others each have a double and a single bed. All the bedrooms here have their own *en suite* facilities and television sets.

Nearby: There is much to do and see in this part of Cumbria, especially if you like walking, riding or water sports. Ullswater is a few miles away, as is Haweswater Nature Reserve. Up the road is the pretty village of Askham which lies next to the huge Lowther Park with its deer park and nature trails. It also has an adventure playground and a miniature railway. A sprint down the motorway will take you close to all the other tourist attractions of the Lakes – Grasmere, Ambleside, Coniston, Windermere and so on.

✘ Dinner (7pm)
   Children: half portions
   Best Room Rate: £30 per person
✔ Best Bargain Break: £99 per person, 3 days - dinner, b&b
   Children: free up to 6 years; half price from 7 to 16
   Facilities: 2 cots and 2 high chairs
   6 rooms, 1 family
   Open 1 March to 30 November
🅿 Ample

HEVINGHAM, NORFOLK   Map 6
Ⓗ℗ **MARSHAM ARMS HOTEL, Holt Road**
Tel: 01603 754 268
On the B1149 north of Norwich.

This appealing inn, smartly decorated under its tiled roof, stands in the countryside about seven miles from Norwich and was originally a hostel for farm labourers, built in the 19th century. The wooden beams and large open fireplace survive from the original design.

The building has been extended over the years to provide better facilities for families, who are welcome to use a spacious and nicely furnished room away from the bar. It is a no-smoking area. There is an excellent range of food on offer, and a good choice of real ales.

There is a terrace with tables and chairs and wooden benches – a pleasant place to sit in the sun with a meal or a drink. Alongside there is a children's play area, which is surrounded by trees.

Eight comfortable rooms are situated in a smart single-storey block alongside the pub. These are spacious rooms, equipped with either twin or double beds and sofa beds. They can accommodate a family of four without any strain and offer very good value for money.

The Marsham Arms, out in the countryside but so close to Norwich, provides excellent all-round facilities for families.

Nearby: The Broads are quite close as is the Norfolk coast. There are many tourist attractions within reach including Thrigby Hall wildlife gardens, Blickling and Felbrigg Halls and the Shire Horse Centre.

....

✕   Bar Snacks (11am to 2.30pm and 6pm to 10pm) £1-12:
      Dinner (7pm to 10pm) £12
      Children: own menu, half portions
      Best Room Rate: £30 per person
      Children: free up to 5 years
      Facilities: 2 cots and 3 high chairs; baby-listening system
      8 rooms
      Open all year, except Christmas
♀   Ale: Adnams, Bass, Greene King
P   Own car park

NR HOLSWORTHY, DEVON   **Map 1**
Ⓢ **GLEBE HOUSE, Bridgerule**
Tel: 01288 381 272.
Off the B3254 south east of Bude

....

We have known the Glebe House properties for many years and spent an extremely enjoyable Christmas there a few years ago. All the buildings are Grade II listed and are in immaculate condition. Nevertheless the owners, James and Margaret Varley, have a continuous programme of refurbishment and redecoration under way. For example, the car park has been moved to a new position more convenient for guests.

The focal point of the estate is Glebe House itself; a lovely stone house built in 1800. It was once a vicarage and the regular proportions are as pleasing to the eye as the clematis that clings to the mellow stone walls. This is the Varleys' home but the cellars have been converted into a small, well stocked, bar and alongside is a pleasant restaurant which is open three times a week. Mrs Varley used to run her own outside catering business and offers a wide range of interesting dishes. Childrens meals and vegetarian dishes are also available. Here also there is a games room which has table tennis and a small snooker table.

The cottages have been formed from the original farm buildings and the original features have been retained wherever possible. The Old Stables still has its studded wooden door and the wooden pillars and beams; the Granary and the adjoining Little Barn have spacious open-plan living rooms on the upper floor, very appealing rooms with their colourwashed stone walls and their wooden rafters. Connecting doors between these two cottages enable them to be rented together by large family groups. Each cottage has a Minstrel's gallery above the living room and each contains twin beds and an en suite shower room in addition to the main bathroom.

On our Christmas visit we rented the single storey Forge, which has now acquired an upper floor and has become two cottages (The Gamekeeper's and The Poacher's) one of which sleeps four people and the other five. Each has a four poster bed and a whirlpool spa bath. The conversion has been done with such skill that you cannot see the join; it is indicative of the owners' care and attention to detail.

The cottages are furnished to an extremely high standard; the accent is on comfort and style and every detail is taken into consideration. You will find everything you need and any cook would be happy to work in the well-equipped kitchens.

There are several acres of grounds with stately trees at both ends of the estate and extensive lawns where you can play badminton or croquet. A children's play area has been created with swings, a wooden playhouse and a slide. Nearby there is a barbeque for al fresco meals during those long summer days. There is woodland to explore – it is a wonderfully relaxing place to be

Glebe House offers some of the best self-catering accommodation we have seen; it is in a delightful spot, with a profusion of wildlife, a few hundred yards from the River Tamar, and has many attractions in the vicinity.

Nearby: Sportsmen are well provided for; there are three golf courses within a short drive, stables, tennis and squash courts, indoor swimming pools and fishing facilities (river, lake and sea) all readily available. The sandy beaches to the west are reached in minutes and to the south are the rugged attractions of Dartmoor. Sightseers can head for Clovelly, Tintagel Castle, Pencarrow, Wesley's Cottage and Dobwalls

Theme Park; nature lovers will enjoy the nature reserve at Braunton Burrows, Tamar Otter Park and the Tropical Bird Gardens at Padstow.

Units: 7
Rent: £195 to £695; a typical rent in May or September would be £250 to £375
Other costs: towel and video recorder hire
Central heating: provided
8 cots and 6 high chairs
Open all year

HOPE COVE, nr KINGSBRIDGE, DEVON　　　　　**Map 1**
Ⓗ **THE COTTAGE HOTEL**
Tel: 01548 561 555　Fax: 01548 561 455
Look for Hope Cove off the A381 and take Inner Hope Road.

A comfortable family hotel which has an idyllic position overlooking two safe beaches, which are protected by a grassy headland on one side. From the terrace and the two acres of sloping garden you look out to Thurlestone across Bigbury Bay. There is a swing in the garden and a good-sized playroom upstairs with table tennis, space invaders, a piano and a wide window overlooking the sea.

We have had several reports about this hotel praising the helpful and hard-working staff, who clearly understand how to look after families. The bedrooms are very comfortable and many of them have balconies overlooking the sea. Of the three lounges, one is for non-smokers. An extensive range of food is available, including a great variety of locally caught fish.

✗　　Bar snacks (12pm to 1.30pm) £2-11
　　Dinner (7.30pm to 8.30pm) £18
　　Children: own menu, half portions
　　Best Room Rate: £39 per person
✔　　Best Bargain Break: £35 per person per night - dinner, b&b

Children: from £6 to £14
Facilities: 6 cots and 6 high chairs; baby listening system
35 rooms, 5 family
No credit cards accepted
Closed January
🅿 Own car park

ILKLEY, WEST YORKS
® BETTYS CAFE TEAROOMS, 34 The Grove
Tel: 01943 608 029
In the town centre

Map 9

This busy and cheerful tearoom, like the other Bettys (qv Harrogate, Northallerton and York), is immediately appealing, with its marble topped tables, basket-weave chairs, pot plants and delightful collection of teapots on shelves around the walls. There are real flowers on the tables and the tea is also made from real tea leaves; there is a wide selection, as there is of coffee.

The long room has windows down one side which makes it a bright and airy place; and those adjectives might also apply to the staff, who cope with the demands of a busy cafe with great charm.

Above all, the Ilkley tearooms welcome families, providing an interesting children's menu and superb mother and baby facilities, with a playpen, changing mat and chair in the Ladies and eight high chairs in the restaurant. Most of the cafe is no-smoking.

✗ (9am to 6pm) £2-8: Swiss rostis, Yorkshire rarebits, Masham sausages, omelettes, fillet of haddock with chips
Children: own menu
Open every day except Christmas Day and New Year
🅿 Public car park at rear

KETTERING, NORTHANTS   **Map 7**
Ⓟ TELFORD LODGE
Tel: 01536 310 082

One mile south-west of Kettering, on the A43 close to the junction with the A14. Follow signs to Telford Way Industrial Estate

....

If you are haring along the Al4 and you and your family need a break, the Telford Lodge, a purpose-built and very spacious pub and restaurant, might be the right place for you. It's a well-designed and functional building which is open all day and every day and provides food, including children's menus, from 11.30 in the morning until 10 o'clock at night. And, if you want to break your journey overnight, there is a Travel Inn alongside – one of Whitbread's hotels with reasonably priced rooms.

The restaurant is large and bright, broken up by brick pillars here and there and with wide windows on to a terrace. There is a raised dining area at one end. Plenty of high chairs are provided and there are, in these politically correct times, both mother and baby and father and baby rooms.

Alongside the restaurant there is a huge indoor play area (Charlie Chalk's Fun Factory) which contains an amazing array of playthings – heaven for children, who must be supervised by their adults. Up above there is an adventure playground with a multitude of rope swings, scramble nets and other things on which to climb, jump and swing.

In addition to the restaurant, there is an equally spacious bar area, comfortably furnished. bright and appealing. Laid out on two levels, the screens and the wooden panelling make it a congenial place to settle; it has the atmosphere of a busy brasserie.

If it's a pleasant day, you can sit on the paved terrace at the front of the pub. There is an enclosed play unit for children and it has a safe surface.

....

✕   (11.30am to 10pm) £2-8: a range of hot and cold food
       Children: own menu
♀   Ale: Boddington's and guests
🅿   Loads

NR LICHFIELD, STAFFS   **Map 4**
℗Ⓗ FRADLEY ARMS
Tel: 01283 790 186

Just off the A38 north of Lichfield. Heading north, turn off to Fradley (not Fradley Park), and follow the signs to the Fradley Arms. Heading south, turn left before the Lichfield exit.

The large and stately, cream-painted building is clearly visible from the A38 and thirty bedrooms are housed in the well-designed brick Lodge alongside.

Most of the rooms can accommodate a family at a very reasonable price - under £50 during the week.

The pub itself has a charming garden at the front where you can relax on the lawn, shaded by oak trees and a weeping willow. There is another garden at the side which is mostly given over to a children's play area. The children can also have plenty of fun in the indoor Captain Coconuts which is packed with slides, chutes, ball ponds and so on.

The family dining area has many high chairs and is primarily no smoking; it's a substantial room with wood-panelled walls and displays of dried flowers and china plates. The rest of the pub is in a similar style, wisely broken up into a series of booths and smaller rooms. There are padded settles and good wooden chairs.

✗   Food (12 to 9.30pm Sunday to Thursday; until 10pm weekends) £2-9: home-made fish & chips, cajun chicken, prawn platter, steak
        Children: own menu

♀   Ale: Bass, Tetley

NR LINGFIELD, SURREY   Map 3
Ⓟ **RED BARN, Blindley Heath**
Tel: 01342 834 272
On the B2029 near Lingfield

....

An old farmhouse, a lovely brick building with a tile-hung upper storey, and a splendid old barn have been used as the core of this substantial pub, which has excellent facilities for families.

The large family dining room is a fine sight with its wooden beams and pillars, and one end sits under a vaulted wooden ceiling and has a large brick fireplace. There is a little play area with a slide, an amusement machine, Lego etc. This is a no-smoking area and there are plenty of high chairs available, plus a nappy changing facility.

The main part of the pub comprises a long bar with many comfortable chairs and benches. The barn has been turned into a huge dining area and has a remarkable interior with old wooden pillars and and cross-hatched beams under its vaulted roof; there are farm implements and horse brasses on the walls, colourful prints, stags' heads and sets of antlers, wooden pews and dressers and a large fireplace.

The garden is delightful, with fine flowers and an enclosed lawned area with bench tables and a large adventure playground for the children.The pub is open all day and food is available at all times.

....

✕   Food (11.30 to 10pm; Sunday from noon) £2-8: a range of hot and cold food
      Children: own menu
♀   Ale: Boddington's and guests
🅿   Own car park

LONDON

....

Some years ago we stopped making recommendations for our capital city. On the one hand London is so busy and congested that it is not to every family's taste; on the other hand, if you are having a holiday or a day out in London and need a family restaurant or mother and baby facilities, the easiest option is the nearest large department store.

However, we have long been fans of the Browns Restaurant group, which has been represented in the *Family Welcome Guide* since the early 80s. Therefore, we are happy to recommend their London outlets, which offer excellent facilities for families.

LONDON W1
Ⓡ **BROWNS, 47 Maddox Street**
Tel: 020 7491 4565

....

Just off famous Bond Street, the location for art dealers and couturiers of varying repute, Browns is laid out in a modified L shape. You enter a long and narrow room with a lofty ceiling which is interrupted by a substantial skylight. This gives plenty of light to the room which is festooned with potted plants. The long curved bar is here and stairs lead to a small balcony containing three tables under the skylight.

The majority of the restaurant tables are at the far end of a spacious room with a large window and a number of mirrors on the walls. There are padded benches, wood panelling here and there, and another skylight. An unusual feature is the presence of two small dining rooms just off the main eating area. One of them can sit six people and the other three people: pleasant for a small family party or a tete-a-tete.

There are a couple of high chairs and a well equipped mother and baby room (it doubles as a toilet for the disabled).

....

✗   (noon to 10pm) £4-17: moules mariniere, steak and mushroom and Guinness pie, gigot of lamb, steak frites, mushroom Stroganoff
Children: own menu

LONDON WC2
® BROWNS, 82 - 84 St Martin's Lane
Tel: 020 7497 5050

....

Next door to the Albery theatre and in the heart of London's theatreland, Browns occupies a substantial late-Victorian building, which used to house the City of Westminster's County Courts. The four Court Rooms on the first and second floors can be hired, and very impressive they are too – especially Court 1 with its high ceiling and its oil paintings of legal worthies.

The bar and restaurant cover an enormous amount of space on the ground floor of the building. The bar itself is well over a cricket pitch in length, with seating areas around it, including a raised area by a large window which overlooks St Martin's Lane.

The restaurant is divided into a number of open plan rooms on different levels. The familiar Browns' decor is used to good effect: cream walls, wood panelling, padded benches along the walls, wooden tables and bentwood chairs, long mirrors, skylights and a splendid selection of potted plants. It's a relaxed atmosphere, aided in no small way by the youthful and helpful staff.

Families are looked after well: many high chairs are made available and there is a well-equipped mother and baby room at the rear of the restaurant. Two children per adult can eat free of charge – as long as the adult is choosing from the a la carte menu. The two course lunch (from noon until 4pm every day) is excellent value at a fiver, and you can have a pre- or a post-theatre dinner for just under a tenner (two courses).

Like all the other Browns restaurants this is a family friendly place which offers first rate facilities and value for money.

....

✗   (noon to midnight) £4-17: fish soup, whole roast sea bass, confit of duck, calves liver, pasta carbonara
Children: own menu

LONDON, SW13
® BROWNS, Castelnau
Tel: 020 8748 4486
On the south side of Hammersmith Bridge.

This large Victorian building has seen many changes since its former days as a conventional pub; it had a regrettable period as a bar for yuppies (remember them?) and remained in the doldrums for many years.

The Browns group has now taken it on and has transformed it into an attractive bar and restaurant which appeals to a wide clientele, including families. Several high chairs are made available and there is a mother and baby room.

It is an appealing building and the Browns designers have enhanced its charms. The bar has wide windows and the Lloyd Loom chairs give it a distinctly colonial look, aided by the potted and hanging plants, the ceiling fans and the skylight above the serving area.

The extensive dining room is in the same relaxing style. One part of it has a wall of windows which overlooks the terrace (where there are more tables) and the tree-fringed garden beyond. An arbour, with seating for around 50 people, is a pleasant place to be on a summer day. The dining room then extends towards the back of the building - though, strictly speaking, it used to be the front since it looks down Castelnau to the bridge.

This is a welcoming restaurant, with an agreeable atmosphere, in a charming area of London.

✕　　(11am to 11.30pm) £3-17: moules mariniere, roast rack of lamb, vegetable tarte tatin, calves liver & mash, swordfish steak
Children: own menu

GREATER LONDON - KEW
® BROWNS
Tel: 020 8948 4838
On Kew Road at Kew Green

This new branch of Browns is just a short walk from the enchanting Kew Gardens and occupies a pleasant Georgian building which has seen a number of businesses come and go. It was once the Coach and Horses Hotel (now opposite), has housed a butcher's shop (you can still see the hooks in the restaurant), a wine bar called Pissarro's and so on.

The main dining area has cream painted walls, floor to ceiling windows which overlook the street, and the familiar and congenial Browns' decor of wooden floors, ceiling fans, potted plants, padded benches and bentwood chairs. It is a relaxing place and a number of other smaller rooms ramble around the old building: there is a raised dining room, a smaller room which has views of the Green, and a very agreeable little drinking area which will hold a mere eight or nine people.

At the back of the restaurant you will find a small paved courtyard, with a few tables and chairs – a good spot to be on a summer's day.

In accord with Browns' policy, there are several high chairs, a mother and baby room and a children's menu. If you are visiting Kew Gardens, this is the place to come and revive yourself and the rest of the family.

✗ Food (11am to 11.30pm) £4-17: moules mariniere, steak and mushrrom and Guiness pie, vegetable tarte tatin, grilled swordfish, steak frites
Children: own menu

LOOE, CORNWALL   **Map 1**
Ⓗ HANNAFORE POINT HOTEL
Tel: 01503 263 273

....

This substantial hotel has a wonderful location high above Looe and has a notably traditional seaside look. From its balconies, terraces and public rooms guests have superb views of Looe Bay and across Whitesand Bay to the distant Rame Head. To the left and within easy walking distance is Looe's sizeable sandy beach.

There is a great array of facilities at the hotel including an indoor heated swimming pool, a spa bath, a sauna and a steam room, a squash court and a gymnasium. Many of you may prefer to contemplate the views from the terrace and the bar.

We looked at one of the family rooms which has plenty of space - even with a king-sized bed installed. There are bunk beds in an adjoining room and it has the great bonus of a balcony.

Nearby: you can visit St George's Island and walk the South Cornwall Coast Path. Looe is still an important fishing port and a lively resort and its Old Guildhall Museum is worth a visit. Dobwalls Theme Park, Lanhydrock House, Restormel Castle and the Monkey Sanctuary are within easy reach. Golfers are well-catered for with several excellent courses nearby including Lanhydrock and the championship lay-out of St Mellion.

....

✗   Bar snacks (12 to 2pm & 6pm to 9pm) £2-5: baked potatoes, sandwiches, ploughman's;
Dinner (7pm to 9pm) £17: smoked mackerel, roast pork, pudding & cheese
Children: own menu
Best Room Rate: £35 per person
✔   Best Bargain Break: £99 to £130 per person, 3 nights - dinner, b&b
Children: under 5 free; 5 to 14 years £10, b&b
Facilities: cots, high chairs and baby listening
37 rooms, 8 family
Open all year

NR LYMM, CHESHIRE   **Map 8**
Ⓟ **THE SARACEN'S HEAD**
Tel: 01925 752 051
On the A6144 just north-east of Lymm at Warburton

This is a very cheerful pub with lively floral wallpaper, wood panelling and padded settles all around the walls. It was very busy with families when we called in one summer Sunday afternoon and has all the necessary features to cope with them: a children's menu, high chairs, baby changing facilities, a separate family dining room and an extensive play area for the younger fry. The garden is large and has a playground and the indoor Adventure Island has a whole host of equipment.

The Saracen's Head has the look of a traditional village pub, its white-painted facade covered in Virginia creeper and it has the additional attraction of providing the full range of facilities - not just for families but also for unencumbered adults who have their own areas of the pub in which to relax.

✕   Food (12 to 9.30pm, Sunday to Thursday; until 10pm at weekends) £2-9: prawn platter, cajun chicken, steak, home-made fish & chips
        Children: own menu
♀   Ale: Boddington's, Tetley

LYNMOUTH, DEVON   **Map 1**
⊕ TORS HOTEL
Tel: 01598 753 236
On the A39.

....

The hotel stands prominently over the pretty seaside town of Lynmouth, and from the terrace and the various public rooms, and most of the bedrooms, you have splendid views of the sea and the harbour.

The hotel has been refurbished and the bars and the restaurant are very smartly and comfortably decked out. There is a table tennis room at one end of the hotel and a pool table in another games room. Outside, the hotel has several acres of woodland in which to relax, and a heated swimming pool.

....

✗   Bar snacks (12.30pm to 1.45pm) £2-5; £10 for 3 courses
Dinner (7pm to 8.45pm) £23
Children: own menu, half portions
Best Room Rate: £35 per person
✔   Best Bargain Break £40 per person per night – dinner, b&b
Children: babies free; £5 thereafter
Facilities: several cots and high chairs;
4 baby-listening lines and 2 baby alarms
35 rooms, 5 family, 2 interconnecting
Closed 2 Jan to 1 Mar
🅿   Own car park

LYTCHET MINSTER, NR POOLE, DORSET   **Map 2**
Ⓟ **BAKERS ARMS**
Tel: 01202 622 900
On the A35 at the roundabout where it meets the A351 west of Poole

....

The Bakers Arms was listed in several early editions of *The Family Welcome Guide* and is now a part of the Brewers Fayre chain.

It offers considerable facilities for families within its spacious rooms: there is an indoor play area with lots of equipment, nappy changing facilities, plenty of high chairs and a large outdoor adventure play ground, which is safely enclosed and has a bark surface.

The pub is open throughout the day and food is available for most of the time. The family dining area is spacious and is, of course, a no-smoking room. The interior is welcoming and is sensibly divided up into a number of small rooms and alcoves, with wooden tables and pews, padded chairs and benches. The brick walls, glass screens and wooden pillars add to the agreeable atmosphere.

....

✕   Food (11.30 to 10pm; Sunday from noon) £2-8: a range of hot and cold food
       Children: own menu
♀   Ale: Boddington's and guests
🅿   Own car park

NR MAIDENHEAD, BERKSHIRE   Map 5
Ⓟ EAST ARMS
Tel: 01628 823 227
From junction 8/9 of the M4 follow the A404M and then the A4130
for Henley and Hurley

The core of this pub is a roadside inn, not far from Temple Golf Club. The facade is pleasant enough in its standard black and white trim and it does not suggest the massive family pub that lies behind it.

The bar area is set out at the front in various alcoves with padded settles and there is a snug room with an open brick fireplace; beyond it you will find an area with a pool table and darts. To one side there is a room for adults, quiet and soberly decorated, it's just the place for a relaxing drink and a chat.

However, this is very much a family pub and there are a number of dining spaces - with all the accoutrements that a family requires, including high chairs, a children's menu and baby-changing facilities. A skylight covers one of the rooms and alongside is a large, high-ceilinged area; with its tiled floor, pale-green decor, windows with coloured glass and ceiling fans we got distinct echoes of the Raj: 'Come you back to Mandalay, where the old flotilla lay'.

Outside, the paved terrace is a nice place to sit on a summer day and it overlooks the playground and the garden which has an array of bench tables under umbrellas. The children can also enjoy all the play equipment in the indoor Adventure Island, which has a snack bar.

✗   Food (12 to 10pm, Friday and Saturday; until 9.30pm otherwise) £2-9: steak, cajun chicken, prawn platter, home-made fish & chips
Children: own menu
Ale: Boddington's, Greenall's

MALMESBURY, WILTS   **Map 2**
ⒽⓇ OLD BELL HOTEL, Abbey Row
Tel: 01666 822 344
In the town centre.

....

The Old Bell was recommended in the first edition of the *Guide* in 1984 and this delightful and historic hotel is now in the care of Nigel Chapman and Nicholas Dickinson who run a select group of hotels (see the entries for Bradford-on-Avon, Fowey and Moonfleet). A great deal of refurbishment has been done over the last year or two, and one of the laudable aims is to offer good facilities for families.

Malmesbury is a charming town and one of the oldest in England (its charter dates back to 930). The hotel stands in the shadow of the famous Norman abbey and was originally built as a hostelry in 1220 by the Abbot, Walter Loring. The mellow stone of the facade is a delight and the interior of the building is spacious and has an ageless charm. For example, the Great Hall still has its 12th-century fireplace, sturdy wooden pillars and heavy ceiling beams, and the effect is complemented by the old wooden settles and tables. Bar meals are served in these wonderful surroundings, and the dishes on offer are not only imaginative but also very good value. That goes for Sunday lunch, too, at £16 for three courses.

Adjoining the Great Hall, there is a splendid lounge with large and inviting sofas (and a piano), and residents can use a more secluded room or the library.

The dining room, built at the turn of the century specifically as such, is imposing. A huge bay window at one end, and other windows opposite, give ample light. The Edwardian chandeliers and oil paintings add to the congenial atmosphere.

The bedrooms are all appointed with style and comfort foremost in mind. Many of them at the front of the hotel, including a family suite, have views across the roofs to the countryside beyond. Young children are well provided for. The Den is their play room – great fun with its murals of animals and of Mowgli, and with plenty of toys and a blackboard – and it is manned from 10am to 6pm every day. There is a children's garden with swings and a climbing frame.

The main garden, its lawn and flower beds well sheltered, looks down to the River Avon, and there is a gazebo at one corner.

The Old Bell is an inviting hotel which offers a warm welcome to families.

Nearby: The town is charming and the Cotswold villages are within easy reach. Westonbirt Arboretum is very close, as are Corsham Court, Bowood House and Lacock Abbey. Bath, Stonehenge, the Avebury stone circles and Longleat are not too far away.

....

✗   Bar snacks (10am to 3pm and 6pm to 10pm) £3-7: Welsh rarebit with ham, black pudding with fried onions, duck liver parfait, marinated salmon, smoked chicken & avocado salad;
Dinner (7.30 to 9.30pm) £20: tartare of salmon, venison faggots, pudding or cheese
Children: own menu
Best Room Rate: £43 per person

✔   Best Bargain Break: £165 per person, 3 nights, dinner, b&b
Children: babies free; nominal charge thereafter for breakfast
Facilities: 10 cots and 6 high chairs;
baby-listening system
31 rooms, 4 family
Open all year

♀   Ale: Smiles, Wadworth's

🅿   Own car park

MAWGAN PORTH, CORNWALL   **Map 1**
Ⓗ⑤ BEDRUTHAN STEPS HOTEL
Tel: 01637 860 555
On the B3276 – the main coast road from Newquay to Padstow.

The hotel has won many awards over the years, not least from the *Family Welcome Guide*, and has attracted a great amount of coverage from the media. Our recent visit, toward the end of the summer season, confirmed that such attention is richly merited – there was no sign of wear and tear, the hotel was in pristine condition and the staff as attentive and welcoming as one could wish.

It is a modern and spacious hotel (it takes its name from the array of huge rocks by the beach) and is totally geared to the holiday needs of families. There are masses of cots and high chairs and virtually all the rooms are family rooms with a variety of designs – many have second bedrooms for the children and the suites have sitting rooms; the Seaview Villa Suites have terraces onto the hotel lawns.

The facilities are outstanding and include squash, tennis and short tennis, snooker and pool, table tennis, carpet bowls, a giant chess and draughts set and skittles. The outdoor swimming pool is very spacious (70 x 47 feet) and is set in a lovely secluded garden; and above there is a shallow learners pool and a paddling pool. There is also a sizeable indoor pool.

Other activities include archery, fencing and crazy golf, and there is a well-equipped gym and a health and beauty spa.

The facilities for children are outstanding: as well as the swimming pools there are various play areas (including adventure playgrounds, swings, a bouncy castle and an area for football), children's films etc. The adventure play centre has a ball pool, tube slide, rope ladders and biff bags; it is indoors and is supervised and has a special toddlers' area. To take the younger children off your hands there are various clubs: the Tadpoles, the Minnows, the Dolphins and the Sharks. Teenages have their own club room with a jukebox, table tennis, table football and computer games. The children's entertainment programme is extensive and includes treasure hunts or nature walks, craft workshops, cookery classes and painting. Recent additions to the facilities include a computer café and a family craft room.

The hotel has a farm and a large market garden, so it is not surprising that most of the vegetables and quite a lot of the fruit used are home-grown. The fish is caught locally, and the bread is made on the spot too. As at its sister hotel, the Trevelgue near Newquay (qv), there are some excellent wines at remarkably good prices and a good selection of vegetarian dishes. On our visit we were very impressed with the standard of the food. The hotel provides a range of home-made pureed foods for babies. All round you get astonishing value for money and that is one of many reasons why the hotel has been a constant presence in the *Family Welcome Guide*.

Nearby: You need never leave the hotel, but there is no shortage of outside attractions. Mawgan Porth beach, right in front of the hotel, is safe and sandy, and there are several excellent beaches at Newquay, a busy resort about six miles away. It has an excellent zoo. The Lappa Valley Railway will appeal to many families, as will the Dairyland Farm Park and Trerice, a superb Elizabethan manor house. Bedruthan Steps itself, a National Trust beauty spot, is only a short walk away.

X   Lunch (12pm to 2.30pm) £2-9: buffet;
Dinner (7.45pm to 9.30pm) £14: crab cakes, soup, Thai red chicken curry, pudding or cheese
Best Room Rate: £38, dinner, b&b

✔   Best Bargain Break: £90 per family (4 people) per day - dinner, b&b
Children: a quarter to three quarters of the adult rate; free of charge in some off-peak periods
Facilities: 60 cots and 45 high chairs;
baby-listening system in every room
75 rooms, 70 family, 15 sets interconnecting
Open March to October

♉   Ale: Bass

🅿   Own car park

SELF CATERING AT THE BEDRUTHAN STEPS HOTEL

The Whittington family have a number of houses, cottages and apartments for hire and guests are able to use all the facilities of the hotel. Cots and high chairs are made available, child safety features are very much apparent, and baby sitting can be arranged.

ST MAWGAN, CORNWALL
LANVEAN FARM COTTAGES

St Mawgan is a delightful little village which has a agreeable 16th century pub with a splendid garden and a handsome church. The three cottages have all been converted from stone farm buildings and offer excellent accommodation for families in a quiet setting. They overlook the village and have particularly good views of the ancient church and the surrounding countryside.

Sampson Cottage was a farmhouse and can sleep four people in a double and a twin bedroom. Bryher Cottage can accommodate five people in a double, a twin and a single bedroom and the cot can be put in the double room. It has a spiral staircase. Barn Cottage was converted from a traditional grain barn and has three bedrooms to accommodate six people.

The cottages are all comfortably furnished, attractively decorated and have well-equipped kitchens. Each cottage has its own lawn with a picnic table and a small barbecue. They all have dishwashers.

Units: 3
Rent: £290 to £665 a week
Other costs: none
Heating: central heating and wood-burning stoves
Cots and high chairs provided at Bryher and Barn
Cottages
Open all year

ST MAWGAN, CORNWALL
THE SUMMER HOUSE

....

This modern stone slate house is hidden away in a secluded valley on the edge of St Mawgan and is a five minute drive from the sea; the hotel is a pleasant walk of no more than thirty minutes duration. The house can sleep a family of nine in comfort. It has two huge double-bedded rooms and two twin bedrooms. There is a suitably spacious lounge (with a wood burning stove) and the picture windows give captivating views over the valley and the Menalhyl river.

The very large lawned garden has a variety of impressive trees and is a delightful spot for a family.

The rents range from £470 to £1425 per week.

BODMIN, CORNWALL
GLYNN HOUSE

....

The Whittingtons recently acquired Glynn, and four apartments will be ready for the 1998 season. Glynn is one of the grandest houses in Cornwall; built in the late 18th century, it is Grade II listed and has an imposing Regency facade. Its former owner was Dr Peter Mitchell, the eminent biochemist who was awarded the Nobel Prize in 1978.

The Mistress's Apartment has unrivalled views over the beautiful Glynn Valley and a series of spacious, high-ceilinged rooms with tall shuttered windows. The sitting room has an open fireplace and alongside there is a large kitchen cum dining room. Above is the master bedroom and a twin bedroom.

The Housekeeper's Suite can sleep six people – in a double room which overlooks a walled garden, and two twin bedrooms. The sitting room looks out to the cobbled courtyard and the kitchen opens on to it.

The Butler's Quarters occupy two floors and can sleep six people in one double and two twin bedrooms. The apartment is warm and welcoming and full of character; for example the kitchen has its original 18th century slate floor and appealing pine furniture.

89

The final dwelling to be done will be the Coachman's Apartment which is across the courtyard from the Housekeeper's Suite and will be completed in 1999.

We saw Glynn when it was being refurbished but were able to look at some of the furniture and decorations. We are confident that the finished accommodation will attain the highest standards.

Bodmin Leisure Centre is a five minute drive from the house and tenants of Glynn can use its facilities free of charge.

The rents will range from around £290 to £780 per week, depending on the season.

MAWGAN PORTH, CORNWALL
THE CAPTAIN'S APARTMENTS

The house is a short walk from the hotel and is indeed a former sea captain's residence which was built in the 1930s. From the slate terrace guests have wonderful views of Mawgan Porth beach and the sea. They have the same views from inside the two sizeable apartments, which sleep four people. Each dwelling has a barbecue and a picnic area in the communal lawned garden; and all the facilities of the Bedruthan Steps are a few yards away.

The rents vary from £350 to £945 per week

MELMERBY, CUMBRIA   Map 8
® VILLAGE BAKERY
Tel: 01768 881 515
On the A686 ten miles north-east of Penrith (junction 40 of the M6).

....

This is a most enterprising and picturesque restaurant. Housed in an 18th-century converted barn, it is set in some spectacular Cumbrian countryside where you will find some marvellous views.

The restaurant has stone walls, a stone-flagged floor and a Welsh dresser against one wall. There is a small and elegant conservatory on the front of the building. Upstairs under the wooden rafters the Bake Shop has an excellent range of products and there are several tables here too.

The food is cooked fresh, often using vegetables, fruit and meat from the organic smallholding at the back of the restaurant. The menu is comprehensive: you can enjoy breakfasts (the full breakfast, traditional or vegetarian, will set you up for the day), lunches, savoury snacks, and cream teas, all at reasonable prices. The restaurant has won many awards including Tea Place of the Year.

Mothers with babies can feed and change them in the Ladies, where there is a pull-down shelf and a changing mat.

The Village Bakery is located right by the village green, which stretches away from the front door.

....

✗   (8.30am to 5pm; Sun 9.30am to 5pm) £2-7
        Children: smaller portions
🅿   Own car park

MOONFLEET, nr WEYMOUTH, DORSET   **Map 2**
Ⓗ **MOONFLEET MANOR HOTEL**
Tel: 01305 786 948
Off the B3157 north-west of Weymouth

The hotel was acquired a couple of years ago by the owners of Woolley Grange, near Bradford on Avon, Fowey Hall in Fowey and the Old Bell Hotel in Malmesbury (q.v.). Those splendid hotels provide exceptional facilities for families and we visited Moonfleet Manor when its refurbishment was in full swing and it was obvious that the same high standards would be attained.

The main building is a very handsome Georgian manor house which was restored near the end of the 19th century. It sits by Chesil Beach in a beautiful location.

One of the hotel's virtues is the amount of space available for guests. The sizeable lounge, for example, has elegant cane furniture, which is all part of the appealing colonial look which the hotel now has. It overlooks a terrace, as does the dining room which has a conservatory running along one side. It is a very appealing room and contains some unusual metal furniture.

We looked at some of the newly decorated bedrooms: a delightful double room and a suite, which has the advantage of two sofa beds in the sitting room and could, therefore, accommodate a small family in comfort. Both are on the ground floor and have solid furniture of high quality.

In all there are 14 family rooms at Moonfleet, including three suites in the old Coach House. There is also be a playroom which is supervised by a nanny.

The Verandah, on the second floor, is open throughout the day, and overlooks Chesil Beach. It's great fun, a very effective re-creation of a colonial club room with its wickerwork chairs, wood panelling and palm trees – you might imagine (perhaps after a few gin slings) that you have walked onto one of the sets from "The Jewel In The Crown".

The sporting facilities are exceptional and many of them are housed in the Ball Park which has a squash court, table tennis, a full-sized ing lanes and two bars. There is a pool table, table football and amusement

Blackbeard's Adventure Play Area with a smugglers tunnel and rope bridge, a haunted house, an aerial slide and ball pond. A new 20 metre swimming pool was about to be built when we visited.

Nearby: The huge expanse of Chesil beach is shingle, but nearby Weymouth has a sandy beach and a Sea Life Centre, which will attract the children. In the other direction lies Abbotsbury, with its ruined Abbey and famous gardens and swannery. If you go inland the lovely town of Dorchester is quite close and Thomas Hardy's cottage and the Tutankhamun Exhibition can be seen. If you are in the mood for sightseeing you can visit the country house of Athelhampton, the tank museum at Bovington Camp and Clouds Hill, the memorial to T.E. Lawrence.

✗   The Verandah (10am to 6pm) £4-8: seafood lasagne, Greek shepherds pie, beef tagine with couscous, Thai chicken curry: Dinner (7pm to 9pm) £16: smoked mackerel, medallions of beef, pudding or cheese
Children: own menu, half portions
Best Room Rate: £30 per person

✔   Best Bargain Break: 10% discount for 3 nights
Children: free
Facilities: 8 cots and 6 high chairs; baby listening system
42 rooms, 14 family
Open all year

♀   Ale: Hall & Woodhouse

🅿   Own car park

MOTHECOMBE, DEVON Map 1
Ⓢ **FLETE ESTATE HOLIDAY COTTAGES**
Tel: 01752 830 253 Fax: 01752 830 500
Email: cottages@flete.co.uk
Website: www.flete.co.uk
Off the A379 east of Plymouth. Follow the signs to Mothecombe.

Superlatives flow trippingly off the pen when describing the Flete Estate, which comprises 5000 acres of extraordinarily beautiful terrain: rolling fields and woodland, the estuary of the River Erme with a profusion of bird life, safe and sandy beaches. It is an unspoiled haven of peace and tranquillity.

Three of the cottages sit in a row above the estuary. Flat-fronted and with a tile-hung upper floor, they were once home to the local coastguards and, as one would expect, have clear views of the estuary and the two headlands. Most of the rooms have the same magnificent outlook, as has the terrace, a fine place to sit and doze contentedly. To the right are the private beaches, where families can play and swim in safety and there are also other beaches on the other side of the estuary.

Each of the coastguards'cottages has three or four bedrooms and can sleep six to eight people. The ground floor contains a well-equipped kitchen, a dining room, a sitting room and a study, which can be used as a fourth bedroom. There is a games room with a table tennis table. The cottages, in common with the other properties, have washing machines, dishwashers, micro-waves, freezers, food processors and coffee makers.

Nepean's Cottage, once the abode of one of the estate's game keepers, is a most appealing stone building with arched windows and doors, and dormer windows in the steep slate roof. It sleeps ten people. Inside, there is a spacious sitting room cum dining room, with two twin-bedded bedrooms at one side. Upstairs, there are two twin-bedded rooms and a double. Surrounded by gentle hills and woodland and with its views of the estuary, the cottage is an unparalleled delight.

A large family would be admirably suited by Efford House, a lovely Georgian stone building which offers space and comfort in a series of beautifully proportioned rooms. The seven bedrooms can sleep up to twelve people and there is ample room on the ground floor for everyone. The house has its own table tennis table. Encircled by undulating fields and woodland, the house has an entrancing view to the estuary.

Finally, Pamflete Flat, forms the end wing of a delightful country house in the very heart of the estate and surrounded by a lovely mature garden. Pamflete Beach is a short walk away.

As well as the beaches, guests can roam the 5000 acres of the estate and enjoy all that it offers: the wildlife, the woodland and the flowers. It is an enchanting place where anyone's spirits will be revived.

....

Units: 7 (5 cottages, a flat and a large country house)
Rent: £300 to £1000
Other costs: linen can be hired and electricity is metered
Cots and high chairs are available for all the houses
Heating: electric (Efford House has partial central heating); all the properties have log fires
Open all year

MULLION, CORNWALL   Map 1
Ⓗ⑤ POLURRIAN HOTEL, Polurrian Cove
Tel: 01326 240 421

Follow your nose through Mullion, past the cricket ground and look for the hotel sign on the right.

....

This hotel has a magnificent location high above the sea and the sand, and has undergone considerable refurbishment over the last few years. New facilities include two-bedded family suites and, a great bonus for families, a spacious and well-appointed creche (with an outdoor area) and a resident nanny. Plans for 1998 include a new terrace which will have a barbecue area.

From the expansive gardens below the hotel you will have breathtaking views across the sea and the cove. If it is action rather than contemplation that you crave, there is plenty to divert you: an outdoor swimming pool, a putting green, a tennis court, and a grassy play area with a slide, trampoline, sandpit and swings – all safely enclosed for the peace of mind of parents. Down below is the cove where surfing can be done.

The indoor games area has snooker, bar billiards and table tennis, and a leisure club has an indoor swimming pool with a paddling pool and a mini-gym plus a sauna and a solarium. There is a warm and relaxing atmosphere at this hotel, which has everything necessary for a happy family holiday, including children's outings to local attractions. Self-catering accommodation is also available in the form of eight bungalows and two apartments. The weekly costs vary from £250 to £800.

Nearby: Most of the surrounding land is owned by the National Trust, and there are delightful walks to take. Mullion golf course is just a couple of miles away, and there are many attractions within reach: Goonhilly Earth Station, the Flambards Theme Park, Poldark Mine, the Seal Sanctuary at Gweek and St Michael's Mount.

....

✗   Buffet lunch (12pm to 2pm) £3-9: chicken & chips, cold buffet, scampi, fisherman's pie, lasagne;
Dinner: (7pm to 8.45pm) £18: steamed Helford mussels, soup, roast leg of pork, pudding or cheese

Children: own menu, half portions
Best Room Rate: £35 per person
✔ Best Bargain Break: £105-£200 per person, 3 nights - dinner, b&b
Children: free up to 14 years
Facilities: 20 cots and 10 high chairs; baby listening system
39 rooms, 6 family
Open all year except Jan to mid-Feb
🅿 Own car park

MUNGRISDALE, nr PENRITH, CUMBRIA   Map 8
Ⓗⓢ NEAR HOWE FARM HOTEL
Tel: 01768 779 678
Off the A66 between Penrith and Keswick

Idyllic is the only word which adequately describes Near Howe, a lovely double-fronted farmhouse built of the traditional dark-hued stone of this part of the country. After you have driven up a long and bumpy road you can look back at the moorland which dips and rolls beneath. This is the Mungrisdale Valley over which John Peel and his companions used to hunt.

You will certainly find peace and tranquillity here, not least in the garden which fronts the house. It has an immaculate lawn, is safely enclosed and ringed with trees, and all around is the glorious countryside. It is a wonderful base for a holiday in an area which has so much to offer – fishing, golf, water sports, walking, or just plain relaxing.

There is a spacious and comfortable residents' lounge and a games room with a pool table, toys and records. The attractive dining room was built in the old dairy and through an arch is the bar. The views from the well-furnished bedrooms are grand and there is an excellent family room, with a double and single bed, at one end of the building.

Three cottages can be rented on a self-catering basis. They were converted from an old barn and have stunning views over the fells. Each has two bedrooms and the rents vary from £180 to £250 a week.

Saddleback Barn can sleep seven people and has three bedrooms, all with *en suite* bathrooms. The weekly cost is from £300 to £490.

✕   Dinner (7pm) £10
        Children: own menu, half portions
        Best Room Rate: £18 per person
        Children: half price under 12 years
        Facilities: 3 cots and 2 high chairs
        7 rooms, 1 family
        Open March to November
        No credit cards accepted
🅿   Loads

NR NEWBURY, BERKSHIRE   Map 5
℗Ⓗ BERKSHIRE ARMS
Tel: 0118 971 4114
On the A4 just west of Woolhampton

This is a stately old pub on the main road fronted by a great expanse of lawn with a number of towering trees. By the entrance to the pub is a terrace and inside you will find an impressive amount of space in which all types of customer can be looked after, from the youngest to the oldest. The restaurant is divided up, with areas on different levels providing pleasant surroundings for diners and drinkers alike. The padded settles sit below the wide windows and the decor leans heavily and agreeably on wood panelling and wood and glass screens, with china plates and dried flowers in evidence.

Families have their own dining areas, predominantly no smoking, and high chairs and a children's menu are provided. Children can take advantage of the outdoor playground or the indoor Adventure Island, with its collection of ball ponds, chutes, swings, ladders, etc.

The Berkshire Arms has a lodge with 29 rooms, at least a dozen of which are family-sized - all priced at a reasonable level, under £50 during the week and under £40 at weekends.

✗ Food (12 to 9.30pm, Sunday to Thursday; until 10pm at
weekends) £2-9: home made fish and chips, cajun chicken, steak,
prawn platter
Children: own menu

♀ Ale: Tetley

NR NEWCASTLE UNDER LYME, STAFFS   Map 4
℗ THE SHEET ANCHOR
Tel: 01782 680 804
On the A53 at Whitmore, south of Newcastle under Lyme

Opposite the village hall of Whitmore you will find this smart old inn, painted white and with double gables on its roof.

The two bar areas have oak beams and pillars and substantial fireplaces. Horse brasses and coloured prints decorate the walls and add to the appealing atmosphere. The large family dining area has wood-panelled walls and a conservatory. The facilities for families are comprehensive; lots of high chairs are available, there is a children's menu, a baby changing room and a separate indoor playground, Adventure Island.

The huge enclosed lawned garden is another handsome feature which everyone can enjoy. You can sit in the sun at one of the many bench tables and the youngsters can have their own fun in the playground.

✗ Food (12 to 9.30pm, Sunday to Thursday: otherwise until
10pm) £2-9: prawn platter, home-made fish & chips, cajun
chicken, steak
Children: own menu

♀ Ale: Boddington's, Tetley

NEWQUAY, CORNWALL   **Map 1**
Ⓗ SANDS FAMILY RESORT
Tel: 01637 872 864
On the B3276 Newquay – Padstow road.

....

Familiar for decades to families, the Trevelgue Hotel has been re-named the Sands Family Resort. Naturally, its old slogan of "parents' haven - children's paradise" is just as appropriate. The hotel is strictly for families and is designed to fulfil their every holiday need.

The Sands has a distinctly Mediterranean appearance and the owners have capitalized on this by redecorating the public rooms in the same style. When you enter the bar, you could easily imagine yourself on the Costa del Sol by dint of the stained glass, the archways and the terracotta walls. It's great fun and very welcoming. And the same goes for the dining room, which is done out in a sparkling sunshine yellow; and for the Piazza where lunches, children's teas and dinners are served. The food has a Mediterranean slant too and the wine list is extensive and always includes some real bargains.

The facilities at the Sands are unrivalled for their variety and availability. There are four children's clubs: the under 2s have the Teddies Club with its soft play areas; two- and three-year-olds meet at the Tigers Club, which has plenty of play equipment, toys and games; four- to seven-year-olds use the Terrier Club, which has a softplay adventure trail, a children's cinema, a bouncy castle, and a Wild West area. Finally, the Tarantula Club is for those between eight and fourteen and meets in the games area where there is table tennis, pool, table football and other games. There is also a Hobby Club in the mornings where guests, and especially the children, can have a go at cookery, ceramic and glass painting, T-shirt printing, modelling and gift making. The club leaders organize all sorts of competitions and outings - the boredom factor is unlikely to affect even the most sophisticated of children.

A great array of sports facilities is available, free, to all the guests and includes basketball, tennis, short tennis, squash, racketball, football, croquet, skittles, a nine-hole par 3 golf course, a BMX track, a fitness trail, a gym - and, of course, an outdoor and an indoor swimming pool. So, when your sporting endeavours have left you exhausted and you feel the need to pamper yourself you can have a massage or relax in the sauna and the hydro spa.

Entertainments are organized on most evenings and include quizzes, casino nights, live music, etc. - or you can simply head for the Beachcombers Bar and get outside a few cocktails.

The basic essentials for parents with young children are provided: there is a launderette and a laundry service, baby food preparation rooms, and a shop where you can hire buggies, sterilisers, backpacks, and so on. No need to fill the estate car to overflowing with all those baby accoutrements.

The Sands offers great value for money and has won plaudits and awards galore, and deservedly so. It is certainly one of the most family-friendly hotels we know.

Nearby: The busy resort of Newquay is just down the road and has safe, sandy beaches. It is one of the main surfing centres in Britain. The children may want to visit the zoo, the Dairyland Farm Park and the World in Miniature; the Lappa Valley Railway and the lovely Elizabethan house at Trerice are within easy reach.

....

✗   Bar lunch (12pm to 2pm) wide range of hot and cold dishes; Dinner (7.30pm to 9pm) £10: grilled mackerel fillet with red onion salsa, charcoal grilled steak, sticky toffee pudding
           Children: own menu
           Best Room Rate: £35 per person (half-board)

✔   Best Bargain Break: £35 per person per night - dinner, b&b
           Children: varies from free to 33% discount
           Facilities: 70 cots and 70 high chairs;
           baby-listening
           70 rooms, 60 family
           Closed Nov to Mar

P   Own car park

NR NEWTON ABBOT, DEVON

Ⓟ **COOMBE CELLARS, Combeinteignhead**

Tel: 01626 872 423

West of Newton Abbot off the A380

Map 1

....

This substantial old pub, smartly painted white and with its facade splashed bright with pots and baskets of flowers, has a memorable location at the edge of the Teign estuary. From the pub's wide windows and its terraces you can view the water and the abundance of bird life. The bar area has a low ceiling of wooden beams and a number of padded wall benches, where you can sit and admire the view. A lounge area has some easy chairs placed by a sizeable fireplace with a wood-burning stove.

The restaurant extends around the seaward side of the building. There is wood panelling in evidence, padded settles and a central brick fireplace. The decorations have a nautical theme: ropes, anchors, lifebelts,fishing nets, parts of boats and many prints. Near the family dining area you will find a small indoor play area with a ball swamp.

On a sunny day you have your pick of three terraces: a paved one in front of the car park, one which overhangs the water on the other side of the pub, or the enclosed lawned garden which has plenty of bench tables. A play area has been established here on a safe bark surface and its focal point is a wooden pirate ship; in summer there is also a bouncy castle.

It is a splendid pub with excellent facilities for families, including high chairs and a nappy changing unit.

....

✗   (11.30am to 10pm) £2-8: a range of hot and cold food
       Children: own menu

Ⓨ   Ale: Boddington's and guests

🅿   Lots

NORTHALLERTON, NORTH YORKS   Map 9
® **BETTYS CAFE TEAROOMS, 188 High Street**
Tel: 01609 775 154
On the main street.

....

On the town's main thoroughfare you will find this civilized and charming cafe, the smallest of the celebrated chain of Bettys. The long room is pleasingly decorated and has prints on the walls and a display of teapots on high shelves. The standards are extremely high and the welcome for families is wholehearted.

There are changing facilities in the Ladies (and a playpen) upstairs and, as well as several high chairs, nappies, bibs and beakers will be provided. The infants' and children's menu shows real flair and imagination .

The home-made cakes are hard to resist and there is also a wide range of savouries, grills and sandwiches, as well as an excellent range of tea and unusual blends of coffee.

....

✗   (9am to 5.30pm; Sun 10am to 5.30pm) £2-8: Swiss rostis, Yorkshire rarebits, Masham sausages, haddock and chips, omelettes
      Children: own menu
      Open every day except Christmas and New Year
🅿   On street and car park nearby

NORTHWICH, CHESHIRE   **Map 8**
Ⓟ WINNINGTON LODGE
Tel: 01606 74217
On the A533

....

The smart black-and-white building has an impressive porticoed entrance and masses of space inside. The high ceilings have a number of skylights with coloured glass, fans and chandeliers. In the bar the various lounge areas have comfortable padded settles; prints on the walls and cupboards with displays of china and pewter add to the cheerful ambience.

The Winnington Lodge cultivates the family market and several high chairs are provided in the restaurant, which is divided into three agreeable rooms, wood-panelled and with huge bay windows overlooking the garden. You can sit in the sun on one of the terraces at the back or on the lawn where there is a play unit. The children can also enjoy all the equipment in Captain Coconuts, a large indoor play area.

This is an excellent pub with all the facilities a family could require, and it is open throughout the day.

....

✕   Food (12 to 9.30pm, Sunday to Thursday; otherwise until
       10pm) £2-9: steak, home-made fish & chips, cajun chicken,
       prawn platter
       Children: own menu
♀   Ale: Boddington's, Tetley

NR NORWICH, NORFOLK
Map 6
Ⓟ VILLAGE INN, Little Melton
Tel: 01603 810 210
Off the B1108 west of Norwich.

....

This very large pub and restaurant is fully equipped to deal with families, and one of its great advantages is that food is available all day and every day right through to 10 o'clock at night.

The huge bar and restaurant area does not overwhelm you with its size because it is broken up by alcoves and wooden screens; and the wooden tables, padded settles and colourful carpet give a very smart and welcoming appearance to the interior.

The family room is also sizeable and has plenty of tables and chairs and a fine array of play equipment for the children: slides, a Lego table, a rocking horse and a blackboard and balloons for very small children. Outside there is an excellent play unit, and a changing table is provided in the Ladies' toilet area.

When a fine selection of real ales and reasonably priced wines and an uncomplicated menu are added to the comprehensive facilities, this adds up to an excellent (and very popular) family pub.

....

✗ (11.30am to 10pm, Sun from 12pm) £2-8: a range of hot and cold food
Children: own menu
♀ Ale: Boddington's and guests
🅿 Lots

OXFORD, OXON   Map 5
® BROWNS, 5-11 Woodstock Road
Tel: 01865 511 995
On the A34 close to its junction with the A423 and just north of the city centre (near St Giles).

....

This big, bustling restaurant has a simple and effective decor of bentwood chairs and wooden tables, and lots of plants and mirrors. The ambience is that of a cheerful and relaxed brasserie. A large skylight gives a spacious effect to the place, and in summer the entire frontage of the restaurant can be opened.

The menu concentrates on salads, pasta and grills, and offers plenty of things to appeal to a young palate. There are lots of high chairs available; and there are even two mother and baby rooms with changing tables and chairs. The staff make a real effort to welcome parents with young children; indeed people of all ages find a warm welcome. We have always liked this restaurant and it thoroughly deserved its Gold Award in the 1996 edition of the *Guide*.

You can eat breakfast until noon, and the special lunchtime dishes, posted on blackboards, are generally a little cheaper than the usual menu; they generally sell out by 3 o'clock.

The restaurant is very spacious and over half is no-smoking.

....

✗   (Mon to Sat 11am to 11.30pm; Sun from noon) £2-11: pasta with various sauces, fisherman's pie, roast poussin, burgers, steak & mushroom & Guinness pie
Children: own menu, small portions
Closed at Christmas

▣   On street

PEMBRIDGE, HEREFORD & WORCS   **Map 4**
℗ NEW INN
Tel: 01544 388 427
On the A44 between Kington and Leominster

....

This is a quiet and delightful village in lovely surroundings close to the Welsh border, and this marvellous black-and-white 14th-century inn, which was once a courthouse, suits it admirably.

Inside is a marvellous public bar, which looks as though it hasn't changed since the inn first traded, with a flagstoned floor, huge open fireplace, black beams and a curved wooden settle. The lounge where children may be taken is large and comfortable, with inviting armchairs and sofas and some nice wooden tables. There is a terrace with several picnic tables at the front of the pub.

You will find some interesting bar snacks here, plus a Sunday lunch for around £6; and there is a high chair on the premises.

The accommodation includes a family room and the bed and breakfast rate is below £20 per person.

....

✕   (12pm to 2pm and 7pm to 9.30pm) £2-7: beef stew with horse radish dumplings, leek and mushroom croustade, roast duckling, mussels in garlic and white wine, feta and black olive salad

        Children: half portions

♀   Ale: Ruddles and guests

🅿   Own car park

RAWTENSTALL, LANCASHIRE   **Map 8**
℗ OLD COBBLERS INN
Tel; 01706 211 116

Close to the end of the M66. Off the dual carriageway in the direction of Edenfield and Ramsbottom. Turn back on yourself at the first roundabout and take the first on the left

Rawtenstall is renowned for its shoe manufacturing and that explains the name of this stone pub. In front there is a little lawned garden, plus a patio and a children's playground, and a terrace with bench tables.

This is very much a pub for the whole family and it contains, upstairs, one of the biggest indoor play areas we have seen. Adventure Island is an absolute delight for any child. There are also plenty of high chairs, a baby-changing facility and an extensive family dining room.

The pub has a nicely understated look: ochre-coloured walls with many old photographs and other memorabilia, wooden screens and padded benches. For the adults there is a games room with a snooker table.

✕   Food (12 to 9.30pm; until 10pm on Friday and Saturday)
     £2-9: cajun chicken, steak, home-made fish & chips, prawn platter
     Children: own menu

♀   Ale: Greenall's, Tetley

REDDITCH, HEREFORD & WORCS   **Map 4**
Ⓟ **NEVILL ARMS, Astwood Bank**
Tel: 01527 892 603
On the A441, south of Redditch, at the junction with the B4090

This handsome brick-walled pub has been expanded to form a very large family pub and restaurant. Although there is loads of space, the interior has been skilfully divided into a series of smaller, interconnected rooms and alcoves, some on slightly different levels to others. The wide windows, cheerful decorations, wooden screens, coloured lights and prints combine to make it an attractive pub.

   The facilities for families are outstanding and include a no-smoking family dining room with a play area which has a ball swamp and other amusements. There are several high chairs, a nappy changing facility and a children's menu; and food is available throughout the day. The garden includes an enclosed adventure playground for the children.

✕   Food (11.30am to 10pm; Sunday from noon): £2-9: a range
      of hot and cold food
      Children: own menu
♀   Ale: Boddington"s and guests

RINGLESTONE, KENT   Map 3
Ⓟ RINGLESTONE INN AND FARMHOUSE
Tel: 01622 859 900

*Not far from Junction 8 of the M20. Turn on to the A20 and follow signs
to Ringlestone via Hollingbourne*

Built in 1533, the Ringlestone was originally used as a hospice for
monks, but it became an ale house around 1615. The inn has changed
little since then and has its original brick and flint walls, oak beams
and inglenooks. Even the later addition of the dining room has tables
which were specially made from the timbers of an 18th-century Thames
barge.

There is an English oak sideboard which has an inscription, carved
in 1632, 'A Ryghte Joyouse and welcome greetynge to ye all'. This is
as appropriate today as it was three hundred years ago. A right warm
welcome is always available between the hours of 12 and 3pm, and 6
and 11pm, and all day at weekends.

To complement the historic inn there is a beautiful garden, two acres
of landscaped lawns, shrubs, trees and rockeries. A water garden has
four charming ponds linked by cascading waterfalls culminating in a
delightful fountain. The patio outside the restaurant enables diners
and drinkers to enjoy the pleasures of this aspect of the garden, while
closer to the farmland is a hopscotch area which is very popular with
children.

In the words of the landlord, 'children welcome in an adults' playground'. There is a children's licence so that they may go anywhere in
the inn, and a high chair is available.

The inn is immensely popular with visitors from the continent as
well as with people from Kent and the rest of the south-east, for this
really is a place of rare beauty steeped in history. There are only three
buildings in Ringlestone hamlet, of which the inn is one, and the
renovated farmhouse opposite provides three charming en-suite bedrooms as well as extensive dining and conference facilities. The neighbouring Garden Cottage has a family suite.

Lunches in the inn are from a help-yourself buffet with a wide
selection of hot and cold foods; evening meals are served in
the candle-lit restaurant. There are delights in food, beer and wines,

especially country fruit wines, with home-made pies like duck and damson a speciality. There is also a strong belief in Francois Maximilien Misson's dictum, 'Blessed be he that invented pudding'.

....

✗   (12pm to 2pm and 7pm to 9.30pm) £2-10: local smoked trout,
     garlic chicken, beef goulash, lamb and Stilton pie, lasagne
     Children: half portions
♀   Ale: wide selection, e.g. Marston's, Morland's, Theakston's,
     Shepherd Neame, Ind Coope, Burton, etc.
P   Ample

ROCK, CORNWALL   Map 1
Ⓢ CANT COVE
Tel: 01208 862 841.
On the outskirts of Rock (the brochure has a clear map)

....

In 1995 the Hamer family spent a hugely enjoyable Christmas week at Cant Cove. The six houses are kept in immaculate order and everything a holidaymaker could wish for is in place – plus a great deal more. One must reach for the full range of superlatives to do justice to the charms and excellence of Cant Cove. The spacious stone houses lie in an idyllic situation on high ground overlooking the waters of the Camel Estuary with the slopes of Cant Hill on the other side. One of the delights is to sit on the terrace of your house and, as the tide recedes, watch the wrecks of the 19th century ketches which lie in Cant Cove appear.

The six houses can accommodate from five to eight people, are models of good design and nothing is stinted in the way of equipment and furnishings. It is no surprise to learn that Cant Cove has earned the Tourist Board's highest classification: five keys de luxe.

The Old Granary can house a large family in its four bedrooms and has a splendid and spacious lounge with open roof timbers and a Delabole slate floor. French windows lead out to a large terrace with a barbecue and a large garden. The Farmhouse, its walls clad in wisteria, has great appeal. There are three bedrooms, a sizeable lounge with oak beams and a large kitchen with the original stone floor. Both houses have the benefit of a sauna. The other houses also have terraces and gardens, high quality bathrooms, extensively equipped kitchens which include microwaves and dishwashers, and utility rooms with washing machines and tumble driers.

Cant Cove has seventy acres of land, a hard tennis court and golf practice area.

Nearby: Rock is a delightful village and is well known as a sailing centre. Water-skiing is available, there is surf at Polzeath beach, or you can walk along the sands of Daymer Bay or the North Cornwall coastal path. Fishing and pony trekking are both available locally and bicycles can be hired. Golfers have several courses to choose from including St Enodoc's and Trevose. Among the many other attractions within reach are Pencarrow, Lanhydrock, Trerice, Newquay Zoo and Tintagel Castle.

Units: 6
Rent: £310 to £1770 (short breaks available)
Other costs: none
Heating: central heating and log fires
Facilities: Cots and high chairs available
Open all year

Nr ROSS-ON-WYE, HEREFORDSHIRE   **Map 4**
Ⓢ WYE LEA, Bridstow
Tel: 01989 562 880.
Off the A49, just west of Ross-on-Wye.

Immense care and considerable thought has been lavished on Wye Lea, a development of ten cottages and three apartments within an estate of nearly twenty acres. It was completed a decade ago by Mr and Mrs Bateman who live in the attractive sandstone manor house, built in the mid-19th century, which forms the hub of the estate.

There are two apartments on the first floor of the house and the larger one, Wysteria, sleeps three people in its two bedrooms, each of which has its own bathroom or shower room. As one would expect in a Victorian house the rooms are spacious, and they have been decorated and furnished to a very high standard. The second apartment, Peartree, will house two people and both properties have views of the immaculately maintained gardens with their smooth lawns, mature trees and profusion of flowers and shrubs. Many young trees have been planted for the future.

Three cottages have been built from the old stables, a very appealing sandstone building like the main house. Each of the cottages has a double and a twin bedroom (and two bathrooms or shower rooms), a dining room and a sitting room and the exposed beams are offset by the smart decorations and excellent furniture. Nothing has been stinted either in terms of space, decoration or equipment. Each of the properties has plenty of garden in which to laze, and a terrace. Linhay has been designed on one level and is suitable for accompanied disabled guests. It has a lovely enclosed stone terrace, which faces south.

Close by there is a detached cottage, Squirrels, which sleeps six people. There are particularly spacious living areas and a spiral staircase leads up to the three bedrooms and two bathrooms. A large and splendid garden completes the picture.

Bramble Court was built from scratch as holiday accommodation and comprises seven cottages of varying sizes to sleep from four to six people. The building resembles a mews, the walls partly of brick and partly rendered, and the design is nicely completed by a small central clock tower. Each cottage has plenty of space and the beamed ceilings

113

and stylish decorations are instantly appealing. The kitchens, as in all the properties, are superbly equipped; everything a cook would need is provided and everything is laid on to make a visitor feel at home, including two bath or shower rooms per cottage.

Above all, the extra facilities provided at Wye Lea are first class. There is an excellent indoor swimming pool, a steam room, solarium and hydrotherapy bath; adjoining them are a bar lounge and a restaurant which opens every day except Monday and also for Sunday lunches. There are two hard tennis courts, which are floodlit, a croquet lawn, a five-a-side football area, a short mat bowling green and skittles and a 9 hole putting green. Mr Bateman, a keen fisherman, owns a stretch of the Wye River and guests can take advantage of this facility too.

Finally there is a children's play area with a climbing frame, a tree house, swings, ball games and a small menagerie with pygmy goats, donkeys and chipmunks; and an indoor games room with table tennis and other play equipment. There is also a full sized snooker table and a well-equipped fitness centre.

A few years ago we spent Christmas at Wye Lea and had a splendid holiday. The owners have expended considerable skill and imagination in developing their estate; the accommodation and the facilities are superb and the whole atmosphere is instantly and warmly welcoming.

Nearby: You need hardly leave Wye Lea, such are its attractions, but the beautiful Wye Valley also beckons. The Wye Valley Visitor Centre is a good starting point and the ruins of Goodrich Castle are also close at hand. In Gloucestershire you can visit the Wildfowl Trust at Slimbridge, Berkeley Castle and the Dean Forest Railway; over the border in Gwent there is a ring of castles to see and the famous Tintern Abbey. Golf is easily available in the locality as are horse riding, canoeing and clay pigeon shooting.

Units: 13
Rent: £290 to £1170 (short breaks available from £120 for two nights)
Other costs: gas and electricity by meter
Heating: central heating
Several cots and high chairs
Open all year

ROWSLEY, nr MATLOCK, DERBYSHIRE   **Map 7**
® CAUDWELL'S COUNTRY PARLOUR
Tel: 01629 733 185
Signposted off the A6 between Matlock and Buxton.

This is a wonderful place to bring the family for an afternoon out with a difference. The small but immaculate cafe is part of the Caudwell's Mill Craft Centre complex. This features a working 19th-century flour mill, driven by a water turbine, and five craft workshops open to the public where glassblowers, wood-turners and a blacksmith keep alive dying traditions.

The food is almost entirely vegetarian and includes flour from the mill, and everything is prepared freshly every day. No additives are used in the food and every effort is made to use environmentally friendly products: recycled paper, etc. Their policies are to be applauded and encouraged.

The complex is surrounded by lawns and a mill stream idles its way past. It is a peaceful haven away from the commercialism that has blighted so much of beautiful Derbyshire.

✗   £2-4: crofters pie, cream cheese and spinach and mushroom bake, lasagne, home-made pizzas
Children: half portions, own menu on request
Open 10am to 6pm, winter until 4.30pm; closed Christmas Day, Boxing Day and weekdays in January
No credit cards accepted
Unlicensed
🅿   Own car park

ST AUSTELL, CORNWALL   **Map 1**
⊕ CARLYON BAY HOTEL
Tel: 01726 812 304
Off the A390 east of St Austell

....

The hotel was built in 1930 and has a marvellous location in 250 acres of grounds, which include a top class golf course of 6500 yards, and a well-established nine-hole short course. The extensive landscaped gardens are a delight, due in no small part to the excellent climate of the Cornish Riviera, and have marvellous views of the bay. The coastal path, part of the hotel grounds, is a lovely spot to explore.

The facilities here are superb. As well as the golf courses, there are two hard tennis courts and a sizeable outdoor heated swimming pool. Children are catered for with a very well-equipped adventure play ground, which is shaded by lofty trees. If the weather is unkind you can enjoy the splendid indoor leisure centre which has an excellent swimming pool, a children's pool area, sauna, solarium, spa bath and beauty salon. There are two full-size snooker tables, table tennis and a children's play room (during school holidays).

This excellent hotel offers a high standard of service and comfort to give a relaxing and agreeable family holiday. It is good to report that there is an extensive and healthy menu for children and a good choice of vegetarian dishes, all served in the refurbished Bay View Restaurant.

Nearby: The coastline is dotted with lovely sandy bays, including one below the golf course. If you fancy seeing the sights, Charlestown, an 18th-century port, is on the doorstep and has a visitor centre. Other attractions: Restormel Castle, Lanhydrock, the farm park at Bodmin, Dobwalls Theme Park, Trelissick Garden, the Dairyland Farm Park, Trerice and the Newquay Zoo.

....

✕   Lunch (12.30pm to 2pm) £13: duck liver pate, medallions of venison, pudding;
Dinner (7pm to 9pm) £24: mille-feuille of crab & prawns, smoked salmon & scrambled eggs, roast pheasant, pudding and cheese
Children: own menu

Best Room Rate: £76 per person

✔ Best Bargain Break: £152-196 per person, 2 nights, dinner, b&b
Children: from £5 a day to 75% of the adult rate
Facilities: 6 cots and 6 high chairs;
baby-listening system
73 rooms, 3 family, 12 sets interconnecting
Open all year

🅿 Own car park

ST HELENS, MERSEYSIDE   Map 8
Ⓟ THE ROYAL OAK
Tel: 01744 885 437
On the A580 just west of St Helens

....

The Royal Oak is a family-friendly pub and restaurant on the East Lancashire road. Built of stone, the pub has a half-timbered upper storey and the interior is bright and comfortable. A full range of necessities for families is provided: a separate family dining area, plenty of high chairs, a baby changing room and a children's menu.

The family dining room includes a conservatory which leads out to the extensive garden where there are bench tables and a playground. If the weather is unkind the children can have fun in the indoor Adventure Island which has a grand collection of equipment.

Like the other outlets in this group there are areas specifically for adults only and at the Royal Oak it is a spacious upstairs room which also has a conservatory.

....

✘ Food (12 to 9.30pm, Sunday to Thursday; until 10pm
otherwise) £2-9: prawn platter, home-made fish & chips,
steak, cajun chicken
Children: own menu
Ale: Tetley

SAUNTON, nr BARNSTAPLE, DEVON   **Map 1**
ⒽⓈ **SAUNTON SANDS HOTEL**
Tel: 01271 890 212
On the B3231.

....

This large and impressive hotel, prominently situated above the rolling expanse of Saunton Sands, has an excellent range of facilities for families and succeeds in looking after them well.

There is an indoor swimming pool, with a paddling pool for the children, and a sauna; there is a squash court, a mini-cinema, a pool table and table tennis. The sizeable outdoor pool also has a paddling area for children and sublime views over the sands and the sea; there is a putting green, a hard tennis court, swings and a children's play area and a path down to a long stretch of sandy beach. Horse riding, sailing, wind-surfing and fishing can all be arranged by the hotel staff; just down the road is Saunton Golf Club, a splendid links course which offers a stern test for any golfer.

One of the great bonuses of this hotel is the presence of a nanny, who attends from 10am to 5pm every day and until 3pm on Sunday. There are plenty of toys here and lots of organized activities. The bedrooms are comfortable and well appointed, some with little terraces or balconies and many with enchanting views over the bay. There are also fifteen self-catering apartments, many of which look out over the dunes and the estuary. The prices range from £120 to £215 per night.

Nearby: Saunton Sands spreads below the hotel and there are many other fine beaches including Woolacombe and Croyde Bay. Nature lovers should see Braunton Burrows, one of the largest nature reserves in Britain, and the children will enjoy a visit to Exmoor Bird Gardens. They will have fun, too, at Watermouth Castle, and Arlington Court is well worth a visit.

....

✕   Lunch (12.30pm to 2pm) from £11: prawn and crab cocktail, supreme of salmon, pudding and cheese
Dinner (7.30pm to 9.30pm) £23: melon and Parma ham, brochette of monkfish & scampi, pot roast pheasant, pudding or cheese

Children: own menu, half portions
Best Room Rate: £63 per person
✔ Best Bargain Break £125-250 per person, 2 nights - dinner, b&b
Children: free up to 2 years; 60% discount from 2 to 5; 40%
discount from 6 to 11 years
Facilities: cots and high chairs;
baby-listening line for every room
92 rooms, 19 family, 12 suites
Open all year
🅿 Own car park

SOLIHULL, WARWICKSHIRE   Map 4
Ⓟ **THE RESERVOIR**
Tel: 01564 702 220
From junction 4 of the M42, follow the A34 northwards and then the
B4102 to Earlswood

....

The core of the Reservoir is a traditional village pub and it was good to
see that the public bar, recently refurbished, is still in use and has its
own entrance. The rest of the pub has been greatly extended and has all
the amenities a family could need, including plenty of high chairs, baby
changing facilities, a children's menu and loads of space.

There is a terrace at the back and a very agreeable enclosed garden
with many shady trees. The outdoor play area is augmented by the
indoor Adventure Island with an array of equipment and a snack bar.

The spacious interior of the Reservoir comprises a number of
comfortable alcoves with wooden screens and raised areas and there is
a separate family dining room. It is comfortable and brightly decorated
and the many prints on the walls add to the fun.

....

✘ Food (12 to 9.30pm, Sunday to Thursday; until 10pm
at weekends) £2-9: cajun chicken, steak, prawn platter,
home-made fish & chips

Children: own menu
Ale: Greenall's, Tetley

NR SOUTHAMPTON, HANTS   **Map 3**
ⓅALMA INN, Lower Upham
Tel: 01489 860 227
North-east of Southampton, on the A2177 at Lower Upham

This attractive low-slung pub, built from flint and brick, is only a stone's throw from the Marwell Zoo.

The Alma has a sizeable bar area on two levels. The well-proportioned room has bay windows and is nicely furnished with an array of padded settles and comfortable chairs. The no-smoking restaurant area is in the same style and has a wooden ceiling, cheerful lampshades of coloured glass, and wooden pillars and screens.

It is an excellent spot for families, since food is available throughout the day. There are several high chairs and a mother and baby room. In addition, there is a small play area inside the pub and a substantial play unit outside with a safe bark surface. Adults can sit on the lawn alongside or on the small terrace.

✗   (11.30am to 10pm) £2-8: a range of hot and cold food
       Children: own menu
♀   Ale: Boddington's and guests
🅿   Own car park

NR SOUTHAMPTON, HANTS
Ⓟ **WINDHOVER MANOR, Bursledon**
Tel: 01703 403 500
Close to junction 8 of the M27. Follow signs to Hamble

Map 3

....

The original part of the building is a grand, half-timbered manor house which was once owned by one of Britain's great aviation pioneers, Sir Edwin Alliott Verdon Roe.

It now houses a very large pub and restaurant. The sunroom was part of the old building and is a very pleasant spot to have a meal. Off the sunroom, the ground floor is broken up into a number of areas and alcoves on different levels. It is pleasantly decorated with Laura Ashley-style wallpaper, wood panelling, a beamed ceiling and screens of wood and coloured glass.

A children's indoor play area has been made to one side of the restaurant and is complemented by a substantial outdoor play unit with slides and swings. A pretty stretch of lawned garden is shaded by mature trees.

There are high chairs in numbers and a baby changing facility. The pub serves food throughout the day.

....

✗   (11.30am to 10pm) £2-8: a range of hot and cold food
       Children: own menu
♀   Ale: Boddington's and guests
🅿   Own car park

121

STOKE BARDOLPH, NOTTS   **Map 7**
Ⓟ **FERRY BOAT INN**
Tel: 01159 871 232
Turn off the A612 at Burton Joyce and follow the road through Stoke Bardolph

....

The pub has a wonderful location alongside the River Trent and you can sit on the terrace under the trees and look across the water to the fields beyond.

The building has been in position for a couple of centuries and the original part still has its low ceilings and huge wooden beams and substantial pillars. It has now been greatly extended to offer a full range of facilities for families; the sitting and dining areas are made up of comfortable alcoves and skilful use has been made of wood and glass screens. The main bar has a flagstone floor and there is a very extensive family dining area with windows overlooking the river.

At one end of the pub is Adventure Island, whose slides, ball ponds and chutes will keep the children amused for hours. Outside there is another playground in an enclosed lawned garden; and more tables and chairs in a courtyard.

It's an interesting pub in a splendid position with exceptional facilities for families.

....

✗   Food (12 to 10pm, Friday and Saturday; otherwise until
        9.30pm) £2-9: prawn platter, steak, cajun chicken, home-
        made fish & chips
        Children: own menu
Ⓨ   Ale: Greenall's, Tetley

STUDLAND, DORSET   **Map 2**
Ⓗ KNOLL HOUSE HOTEL
Tel: 01929 450 450 Fax: 01929 450 423
Email: enquiries@knollhouse.co.uk
Website: www.knollhouse.co.uk
On the B3351 east of Corfe Castle and north of Swanage.

The Ferguson family have owned the Knoll House since 1959 and adhere to their philosophy of holding the balance between the differing requirements of their guests: on the one hand it has a location and an array of facilities which appeal greatly to families (and it continues to be one of our favourite family hotels), and on the other it also has many regular guests who are unencumbered by children. The philosophy is easy to express but difficult to achieve; in our opinion the Fergusons achieve it with style and aplomb.

Everyone is well looked after here. The children have their own dining room, with decent wooden furniture and cheerfully decorated with animal murals and colourful blinds. As well as their breakfast the children can have their lunch (there is an excellent menu which includes dishes such as grilled fish and roast beef) at 12.30 and are then supervised in the well-equipped play room (Wendy House, playpens, video cartoons, toys, etc) while the parents have their meal in peace. Similarly, children under 8 are not permitted in the dining room at night, but have high tea from 5 o'clock.

The facilities within the hotel and the 100 acres of grounds are extensive and include a heated swimming pool and paddling pool, safely enclosed, with a terrace, lawn and bar; a huge play area shaded by tall pines, with a pirate ship and a wonderful and ingenious 'Hag' adventure playground; and a par-3 golf course and two hard tennis courts. Indoors there are games such as table tennis, pool, table football, etc. Finally the well-designed leisure centre has a small indoor pool, a fitness room with serious equipment, a sauna, steam room and solarium, and a health juice bar. This is primarily a place for adults, but children are allowed in from 11am to midday, and for an hour during mid-afternoon.

There is a feeling of spaciousness in the hotel, not least in the dining room where the tables are set well apart and a wall of windows overlooks the gardens. Similarly, the family suites offer plenty of space, with separate single or twin bedrooms for the children. The location of the hotel, with its expansive grounds, encircled by National Trust land, and with one of the best beaches in Britain on the doorstep, is outstanding. It is a top-class family hotel in a superb holiday area.

Nearby: The beaches in this area are splendid, and indeed the Studland beach, with over three miles of sand, is one of the best and cleanest in Britain. Behind it lies the Studland Heath Nature Reserve. The Swanage Railway is on the doorstep, as is Durlston Country Park and Corfe Castle. Brownsea Island is delightful and has many sandy beaches, too. Sightseers can easily reach the Tank Museum at Bovington, Hardy's cottage and the Tutankhamun Exhibition at Dorchester; and the children will enjoy a visit to the Sea Life Centre at Weymouth and to Monkey World.

✕   Lunch (1pm onwards) £16: hors d'oeuvres, soup, grilled whole local plaice, pudding and cheese;
Dinner (7.30pm onwards) £17: creamed smokies with prawns, roast Dorset lamb, pudding, cheese
Children: own menu in children's dining room
Best Room Rate: £82 per person

✔   Best Bargain Break: £757 (per family of 4)
5 nights - full board
Children: a sliding scale depending on age
Facilities: plenty of cots and high chairs;
baby patrol from 7.30pm to 11pm
80 rooms, including 30 family suites
Closed November to end March

🅿   Own car park

TAUNTON, SOMERSET
℗ BATHPOOL
Tel: 01823 272 545

Map 2

Close to junction 5 of the M5. Take the Taunton road and then the A38 north (towards Bridgwater)

This must once have been a village pub on the outskirts of Taunton; it's a long, low-slung, building with residual charm. It has been transposed into a spacious family pub and restaurant – with some success because it has been designed as a series of small rooms, most of which have low, beamed ceilings.

At one end of the pub there is a conservatory room which overlooks the garden; opposite you will find a snug little alcove with prints and china plates decorating the walls. Further into the pub there is a non-smoking dining area, notable for its green-painted wall panelling and an old Esse cooking range. There are more alcoves and a main dining area with an open fireplace.

For the drinkers a pleasant lounge bar makes up one end of the building. It has brick walls and a high ceiling and, to one side, there is a games room with darts and bar billiards.

The large lawned garden is safely enclosed and has many bench tables. The play area is laid on a bark surface and there is a bouncy castle.

It's an excellent family pub, open all day, and with plenty of high chairs and baby changing facilities.

✗   (11.30am to 10pm; from noon on Sundays) £2-8: a range of hot and cold food
      Children: own menu

♇   Ale: Boddington's and guests

P   Own car park

NR TELFORD, SHROPSHIRE Map 4
Ⓟ **TAYLEUR ARMS**
Tel: 01952 770 335
At Longdon-on-Tern on the B5063 just north-west of Telford

....

The Tayleur Arms has a very smart and appealing look; it's a low-slung village inn with hanging baskets of flowers adorning the walls and surrounded by neat gardens.

Inside you will find a large family pub but it has a contained and cosy atmosphere, divided as it is into different areas with alcoves here and there. The wooden beams and brick walls, which are decorated with prints and china plates, the coloured lightshades, and the big fireplace by the bar make for a relaxing pub.

All the family is welcome and well looked after: the food is available all day, there is a choice of real ales, and high chairs and baby-changing facilities are in place. The children have two well-equipped play areas, both indoor (in a pleasant brick and wood-clad building) and outdoor, while their parents can relax in the lawned garden.

....

✕   Food (12 to 10pm, Friday and Saturday; otherwise until
     9.30pm) £2-9: prawn platter, home-made fish & chips, cajun
     chicken, steak
     Children: own menu
♀   Ale: Boddington's, Tetley

126

THURLESTONE, DEVON
ℌ THURLESTONE HOTEL
Tel: 01548 560 382
In the centre of the village.

Map 1

This has long been a favourite hotel of ours and on our various visits we have always found that the Grose family, who have owned and run this hotel since 1896, when Margaret Amelia Grose took a lease on the farmhouse, get most things right. When we last stayed we had a delightful room which overlooked the gardens and the sweep of Bigbury Bay, and we found the staff as friendly and efficient as always. The food was of excellent quality and cooked with skill.

All this makes a pretty good starting point for a family holiday. But in addition, this hotel, which is in one of the loveliest spots in south Devon, has wonderful facilities, including two hard tennis courts, two squash courts, a badminton court, a swimming pool and a play area with a climbing net, swings, a playhouse and a slide. The well-designed indoor pool has a paddling pool for very young children. There is also a fitness room. With table tennis and snooker, an excellent par-three course at the hotel and golf at Thurlestone, Dartmouth and Bigbury, all aspiring superstars are catered for wonderfully well. Fishing, horse riding and sailing can all be arranged.

On a practical level, playpens are provided at both swimming pools and there is a well-equipped laundry room (washing and drying machines, ironing board and iron). The hotel's Dolphin Club is registered with the local authority.

Good news for real ale fans: the baby-listening service extends to the 16th century village inn next door. Timbers from the Spanish Armada's 'San Pedro' were used to build it.

Nearby: There are plenty of sandy beaches all along this stretch of coast, including one at Thurlestone. Inland, you can visit the National Shire Horse Centre and the Dartmoor Wildlife Centre, Buckfast Abbey and the adjacent Dart Valley Railway, and the castles at Compton and Totnes. There is superb scenery to be enjoyed while walking along the Heritage Coast Path.

✕ Light lunch on the New Terrace (12.30pm to 2pm) £3-9: open
  sandwiches, smoked salmon, sirloin steak, lemon sole and
  French fries
  Dinner (7.30pm to 9.00pm) £24: Parma ham and Roquefort
  salad, soup, medallions of pork loin, pudding and cheese
  Children: own menu, half portions
  Best Room Rate: £55 per person
✔ Best Bargain Break: £48 per person per night - dinner, b&b
  Children: free up to 2 years; £22 to 12 years
  (includes breakfast and high tea)
  Facilities: 6 cots and 6 high chairs;
  baby-listening lines to all rooms
  Open all year (except for a week in Jan)
  65 rooms, 15 family, 3 sets interconnecting, 4 suites
♀ Ale: Bass, Palmer's, Wadworth's
🅿 Own car park

TORMARTON, nr BADMINTON, AVON   **Map 2**
ⓅⒽ **COMPASS INN**
Tel: 01454 218 242

Half a mile north from Junction 18 of the M4 – take the first right turn off the A46 going towards Stroud.

....

This fine old creeper-covered pub of 18th-century origin is in a useful spot – only a minute or so from the motorway. The main bar, with a good selection of real ale, leads down to the food bar. On from there is a huge glass-roofed orangery which is always pleasantly warm and bedecked with hanging plants. Children are welcome in the food bar or the orangery. A patio and a lawned garden offer pleasant spots to sit on summer days.

There is always a good display of food here, from the cold buffet to the daily specials, and it is served seven days a week. There is also an excellent vegetarian menu. The pub is open throughout the day and it is good to report that food is available at all times – from breakfast at 7.30 in the morning until 10.30 at night.

The Compass Inn also has excellent accomodation. The twenty six rooms include six family rooms and two sets of inter-connecting rooms. The cost per person for a room only is £42.

....

✕   (7.30am to 10.30pm) £2-7: fresh poached salmon, chicken curry, dressed crab, lasagne, ratatouille au gratin
        Children: own menu, half portions

♀   Ale: Archer, Bass, Smiles

🄿   Own car park

WATERGATE BAY, CORNWALL   **Map 1**
Ⓗ Ⓢ **WATERGATE BAY HOTEL**
Tel: 01637 860 543 Fax: 01637 860 333
Email: hotel@watergate.co.uk
Website: www.watergate.co.uk
On the B3276 north of Newquay.

This self-contained family hotel is not too far away from the busy resort of Newquay. Not that you need venture there, since there are loads of facilities at the hotel itself, including a sandy beach, part of which actually belongs to the hotel. The coastal footpath runs close by.

The garden has swings, sandpits, a junior 'assault course' and a trampoline, and many activities are organized for the children here and on the beach. In addition, there are Punch and Judy shows, fancy dress parties, swimming galas, table tennis and other sporting competitions, and a clown every week. Adults have dancing and entertainments most evenings.

Indoors, there is a spacious play room for young children with plenty of toys and games, a slide and a pirate ship; this is supervised. Alongside, there is a pool table for older children. The snooker room is confined to adults or children supervised by adults. In addition, there is a tennis court, and a separate sports hall which has skittle alleys, a squash court and a court on which to play badminton, short tennis, etc. adjoins the hotel. There is a putting green on one of the terraces which overlooks the bay and loads of room for families to relax, including a lounge or quiet room for adults only. Aromatherapy is available

The Coffee Shop (open from 10am to 6pm) offers a good range of snacks and dishes of the day. It overlooks the outdoor swimming pool and paddling pool, and alongside it is a small indoor pool.

There are three villas in the hotel grounds, two of which sleep up to five people and the other up to ten. The rents vary from £210 to £965 a week.

Nearby: Newquay itself is a busy and lively resort and, apart from Watergate Bay, there are many safe, sandy beaches in the near vicinity. There are many places to visit. Children will certainly be interested in the zoo, which has a large play area and a leisure centre attached to it,

with swimming pools, squash and tennis courts and a golf driving range.
There is a leisure park at St Agnes, a farm park (Dairyland) near
Newquay and a World in Miniature at Goonhavern, five miles from
Newquay. Add the Lappa Valley Railway and the Elizabethan manor
house at Trerice, and there is something for everyone.

✗   Coffee shop (10am to 6pm) £2-5: ploughman's, plaice
    and chips, filled baked potatoes, pancakes, chicket nuggets
    and chips
    Dinner (7pm to 8.30pm) £16: smoked mackerel pate,
    roast leg of lamb, pudding and cheese
    Children: own menu, half portions
    Best Room Rate: £27 per person
✔   Best Bargain Break: £29 per person per night - dinner, b&b
    Children: free at certain times; 25% of adult rate up to 3 years;
    50% from 4 to 7 years; 66% from 8 to 10; 75% from 11 to 14
    Facilities: as many cots and high chairs as required;
    baby-listening system to every room
    57 rooms, 27 family, 17 sets interconnecting
    Open March to November
⌕   Ale: local brew
🅿   Ample

NR WELLS, SOMERSET   Map 2
ⓗ **GLENCOT HOUSE, Glencot Lane, Wookey Hole**
Tel: 01749 677 160
Follow the signs for Wookey Hole from the A371. In the village look for a pink cottage on the crest of a hill. 100 yards on turn sharp left into Glencot Lane

....

Glencot House is a stylish Victorian mansion set in 18 acres of garden and parkland alongside the River Axe. There is plenty of space for children to play and for adults to relax. It is a quiet and peaceful place.

The building has been faithfully restored during the last few years and the interior decorated and furnished with great care. There is lovely oak panelling throughout the house and fine views through the large mullioned windows. The library is a comfortable and quiet room and the spacious lounge has an unusual patterned wood ceiling; the bay windows overlook the gardens and the river. A charming little bar with a veranda, and a stately dining room, oak panelled and with a splendid chandelier, complete the picture. Antique pieces abound and some discretion must be exercised by younger children. The bedrooms have been furnished and decorated to very high standards, and many of them have idyllic views across the gardens to the water. Plenty of space is provided for guests and especially so in the family rooms.

The extensive gardens are a delight, and guests can fish for trout in the river and play croquet on the lawn. Indoors, there is a small plunge pool and a sauna, a full size snooker table and table tennis.

Glencot House is an outstanding hotel in a superb location, where families are made very welcome.

....

✕   Dinner (6.30pm to 8.45pm) £26
        Children: own menu, half portions
        Best Room Rate: £40-46 per person
✔   Best Bargain Break: £130 per person, 2 nights dinner, b&b
        Children: cots free; extra bed £12
        Facilities: 2 cots and 2 high chairs;
        baby-listening
        12 rooms, 2 family, 1 set interconnecting
        Open all year

WEST ANSTEY, Nr SOUTH MOLTON, DEVON   **Map 1**
ℍ PARTRIDGE ARMS FARM
Tel: 01398 341 217
Off the B3227 east of South Molton.

....

Once a coaching inn, where the last pint was served in 1905, the farm has been in the same family since the early years of this century. It now consists of 200 acres, and sits on the southern slopes of Exmoor. The charming building dates back to the 14th century and has rough-cast walls, painted pale pink, with honeysuckle climbing over them, and the lawned gardens sport several apple trees.

The cosy sitting room has comfortable chairs and a sofa, a large stone fireplace with a wood-burning stove, and paintings of wildlife and hunting scenes adorn the walls. There are no fewer than three charming dining rooms: one has a huge open fireplace decorated with old farm implements and cider jars and the low ceiling is cross-hatched with wooden beams; the next room has another open fireplace and a long wooden table; and the third dining room also contains a small bar, which has been kept as it was in the 19th century.

Everything overlooks the encircling farm land and guests are welcome to wander around among the cows, sheep, geese, dogs, cats and ponies. The farm, by the way, has its own stretch of trout fishing.

All of the bedrooms are pleasing. One has a four-poster, one double bedroom has a separate room with bunk beds, and there is a family room with a double bed and two bunk beds. Most of the rooms have their own bathrooms.

Partridge Arms Farm is run entirely by the Milton family and is a most welcoming place to stay in the heart of the Devon countryside.

Nearby: North Devon and Somerset coastal resorts, including Woolacombe Sands and Croyde Bay. Exmoor is also at your feet – lovely for nature lovers, walkers, and pony trekkers. Also within easy reach: the nature reserve at Braunton Burrows and the Exmoor Bird Gardens; the Maritime Museum at Appledore; Arlington Court; the Dartington Glass factory; Watermouth Castle and the Combat Vehicles Museum near South Molton.

....

✘   Dinner (7.30pm) £10
Children: own menu, half portions
Best Room Rate: £23 to £50 per person
Children: nominal charge up to 5 years; then according to age
Facilities: 2 cots and 2 high chairs
7 rooms, 2 family, 1 set interconnecting
Open all year
No credit cards accepted

🅿   Ample

WEST BUCKLAND, nr BARNSTAPLE, DEVON   **Map 1**
ⓗ **HUXTABLE FARM**
Tel: 01598 760 254
Email: j-payne@huxhilton.enterprise-plc.com
Website: www.huxtablefarm.co.uk
Off the A361 east of Barnstaple. The farm entrance is opposite West Buckland School.

This is a delightful listed building which dates back to the 16th century, a Devon longhouse built of stone and with climbing jasmine over the walls. The house has been restored with care by the owners, and antique furniture complements the original features. The sitting room has fine proportions and looks on to an enclosed garden; it is a comfortable and very inviting room with a wood-burning stove and some pleasing corner cupboards. There are games and a good selection of books. Across the corridor, with its ancient black beams and screen panelling, there is a splendid dining room which has a large open fireplace with a stove, a dresser and a lovely wooden table around which the guests gather to enjoy Jackie Payne's excellent food (and home-made wine). The extensive gardens, and other local sources, provide most of the produce used in the house and the owners take pride in serving home-made wine. Children have their own small dining room for high teas.

There is a games room in the garden, with table tennis, a quarter-size snooker table and lots of toys. There is loads of room for children to play with swings, a sandpit and a Wendy House set up in the garden. There is a tennis court and a sauna and fitness room have been added to the facilities. Sheep are reared on the 80 acres of farm and woodland (home to a variety of wildlife) and children are welcome to help to feed the pet lambs, chickens and goats.

The bedrooms are furnished and decorated to a very high standard and are full of character, with views over the tranquil gardens and encircling countryside. The family rooms are very spacious, especially a secluded one on one side of the house which has a double and two single beds and a bathroom. The two bedrooms in the converted barn also have loads of space. A laundry room is available.

This welcoming and well-equipped farmhouse offers an excellent base for a family holiday.

Nearby: The north Devon coast beaches are close, especially Woolacombe and Croyde Bay, as is the Exmoor Centre near Dulverton. The Tarka Trail runs past the entrance to the farm. There is much else to see: Braunton Burrows, one of the largest nature reserves in Britain; Arlington Court; Watermouth Castle; Exmoor Bird Gardens; the Maritime Museum at Appledore; Dunster Castle, Combe Sydenham Hall and Rosemoor Royal Horticultural Garden.

....

✗ Dinner (7.30pm) £15: herb & liver pate, pork chops in cider and cream, elderflower and gooseberry and almond bake, Devon cheeses
  Children: own menu
  Best Room Rate: £25 per person
  Children: cot £6; extra bed £10
  Facilities: 3 cots and 2 high chairs, baby alarms provided
  6 rooms, 2 family
  Open February to November
  Unlicensed (but take your own wine)
🅿 Ample

WESTONBIRT, nr TETBURY, GLOS   **Map 4**
Ⓗ HARE AND HOUNDS HOTEL
Tel: 01666 880 233
On the A433 southwest of Tetbury.

....

The gardens of this attractive Cotswold stone building, part of which started off as a farmhouse in the early 19th century, are a major attraction: ten acres of delightful gardens, with wide and smooth lawns, beautifully kept flower beds and hedgerows, and grand mature trees. There is also a shady walled garden outside the bar, with several bench tables.

Other facilities include two hard tennis courts, a croquet lawn, a squash court, table tennis and snooker; and down the road is the famous Westonbirt Arboretum, which is open every day of the year.

This is a spacious hotel with plenty of room for families. There is an excellent choice of food on the various menus, which offer good value.

The hotel has two family rooms in the strictest sense, but most of the other rooms can accomodate another bed with ease.

....

✗   Bar snacks (12pm to 2.30pm and 7pm to 9.15pm) £2-10;
Lunch (12.30pm to 2pm) £12;
Dinner (7.30pm to 9pm) £19
Children: own menu, half portions
Best Room Rate: £42 per person

✔   Best Bargain Break: from £106 per person, 2 nights - dinner, b&b
Children: free to age 16
Facilities: 4 cots and 2 high chairs
5 baby-listening lines
30 rooms, 2 family, 2 sets interconnecting
Open all year

♀   Ale: Courage, Smiles

🅿   Own car park

Nr WESTON-SUPER-MARE, SOMERSET   Map 2
℗ **HOBBS BOAT, Bridgewater Road, Lympsham**
Tel: 01934 812 782
On the A370, three miles south of Weston-super-Mare.

When we visited the Hobbs Boat one sunny lunchtime, the garden was packed with children enjoying the adventure playground and the bouncy castle, while the adults looked on and enjoyed their food and drinks.

The large indoor playroom was just as popular and it has an array of things for children to crawl on or under, to ride on and fall on, including a ball swamp. Alongside there is the family eating area (no-smoking) and there are several high chairs and a nappy-changing facility.

The pub is divided up into alcoves and rooms on different levels and this masks its size. Smart wallpaper, richly coloured carpets, wooden furniture and padded benches and chairs make this a comfortable and appealing pub/restaurant with excellent family amenities.

✕   (11.30am to 10pm) £2-8: a range of hot and cold food
     Children: own menu, half portions
♉   Ale: Boddington's and guests
🅿   Own car park

WIDECOMBE IN THE MOOR, DEVON   Map 1
Ⓟ **OLD INN**
Tel: 01364 621 207
North of Ashburton on the minor roads, and can be reached from the A38 or the B3212.

This famous village has a pub to match. It is part of a row of 14th century stone buildings which also house gift and craft shops. It has several rooms with thick stone walls and lots of oak, and the family room has a large open fire, a floor of worn flagstones, oak benches and settles.

Children are also welcome in the long, narrow dining room which has several tables and padded bench seats, and in the other eating areas within the pub.

The way to the car park is not immediately obvious – take the road to the right of the stone buildings and the car park is on your left. Next to it are the delightful water gardens, with several ponds and streams, interspersed with many tables and chairs. You can sit on two islands with gazebos and the whole area has been planted with a variety of pond plants. There is a fish pond and external lighting and a large terrace overlooks the gardens. It must be stressed that parents should keep a close eye on their children.

There's a good choice of food at reasonable prices, with daily specials, several vegetarian dishes and a Sunday lunch for under £6.

✕   (11am to 2pm and 6.30pm to 10pm) £3-11: Moorland smokie, turkey & ham pie, steaks, beef in red wine, bean casserole
Children: half portions
♀   Ale: Theakston's, Flowers
🅿   Own car park

WIMBORNE, DORSET   **Map 2**
℗ **WILLETT ARMS**
Tel: 01202 883 144
Off the A31 at the Merley Bird Gardens roundabout

....

The large family pub and restaurant, built in red brick and tile-hung, is a stone's throw from the Merley Bird Gardens and offers excellent facilities, including many high chairs, baby changing facilities, a children's menu and the availability of food and drink throughout the day.

The cheerful bar area has an array of windows, padded settles, and an open fireplace. The various dining areas are in much the same style with Laura Ashley style furnishings and ceiling fans. One room resembles a conservatory with its walls of windows and massed foliage outside. The family dining room is sizeable and has a Charlie Chalk Fun Factory, with its many playthings for children, alongside.

The patio and garden, safely enclosed, are mostly filled by a play unit and a bouncy castle and were busy with families when we visited.

....

✕   (11.30am to 10pm; from noon on Sundays) £2-8: a range of hot and cold food
     Children: own menu
♀   Ale: Boddington's, and guests
🅿   Own car park

WOOLACOMBE, DEVON   **Map 1**
ⒽⓈ **WOOLACOMBE BAY HOTEL**
Tel: 01271 870 388
In the centre of town.

....

This resort has a magnificent stretch of beach and a lovely setting amid rolling hills. The stately seaside hotel is in pristine condition both inside and out and has some fine public rooms, including comfortable lounges, a welcoming, high-ceilinged restaurant, two bars with real ale, and very agreeable and well-furnished bedrooms.

The array of facilities includes a sizeable indoor pool with paddling pool (galas are organized for children), a steam room, jacuzzi and sauna, three squash courts, including a glass-backed court, table tennis and pool, a very well-equipped fitness room and an aerobics studio, and a very congenial snooker room with wood panelling and a high ceiling (for adults only).

The children have their own spacious play area indoors with table tennis, pool, amusement machines, big-screen videos and lots of organized activities. There is also a creche area for young children.

Everyone can enjoy the large outdoor swimming pool with its flume slide, around which there are lots of reclining seats. In addition the hotel has two hard tennis courts, an expansive stretch of grass in front of the hotel which runs down to the sea, and a play area to the side which has croquet, swingball, and a pitch and putt course. The hotel also has a motor yacht which can be chartered.

All kinds of games and sports are organized during the summer, and entertainments – dances and discos in the large ballroom – are laid on in the evenings.

The Woolacombe Bay is an impressive hotel in a delightful location and has everything a family could desire. For holiday makers who prefer self-catering, the hotel has nearly forty apartments which sleep from two to eight people; the rents vary from £150 to £1205 a week.

....

✕   Bistro (10am to 4pm) £1-4
      Dinner (7.30pm to 9pm) £20 (five courses)
      Children: own menu, half portions
      Best Room Rate: £50 per person

✔   Best Bargain Break: £140 per person, 2 nights dinner, b&b
       Children: free up to 2 years; from £10 to £30 thereafter
       Facilities: as many cots and high chairs as required;
       baby listening to every room
       65 rooms, 27 family, 13 sets interconnecting
       Open mid-Feb to Jan
♀   Ale: Bass
🅿   Own car park

WORFIELD, nr BRIDGNORTH, SHROPSHIRE   Map 4
⊕ OLD VICARAGE HOTEL
Tel: 01746 716 497
Off the A454 east of Bridgnorth

....

This large red-brick house was built in 1905 and is now a small and very comfortable hotel; there are some fine antique pieces, and the walls display watercolours and engravings. The lounge bar, with its wide windows, is a relaxing place to have a drink, as is the splendid and spacious conservatory, full of plants and with excellent views of the countryside. The main dining room looks out to the gardens and there is also a small private dining room.

Hotels often claim that their bedrooms are individually designed, and this is certainly true at the Old Vicarage, where the rooms are very smartly furnished and decorated in fine style. The four rooms in the Coach House merit special mention since they have the extra luxuries of jacuzzi baths and double showers. They are spacious and extremely comfortable and the ground-floor rooms (one of which is superbly equipped for disabled guests) have their own little gardens. The Warlock Room is a family room with a main bedroom and sofa-beds for children in a separate lounge. It is no surprise to learn that the hotel is one of the very few in Britain to be placed in the de luxe category by the AA which has also awarded the hotel three rosettes for its food.

The hotel garden covers two acres, is safely enclosed and has spreading lawns and several mature trees. There is plenty of space for children to play and adults can try their skills on the croquet lawn.

Nearby: South Shropshire is a lovely part of the world with many attractive villages and towns: Church Stretton and the Carding Mill Valley, Clun with its castle, Ludlow and Bridgnorth, which has a motor museum. Within an easy distance you can visit the Ironbridge Gorge Museum, the Severn Valley Railway, Wilderhope Manor, the Safari Park at Bewdley, Wyre Forest and the Aerospace Museum at Cosford. You can play golf at Worfield at half price and Patshull Park is an alternative venue.

✗   Dinner (7pm to 9pm) £25: terrine of Shropshire lamb and apricots, fillet of brill, pudding or cheese
       Children: own menu, half portions
       Best Room Rate: £54 per person
✔   Best Bargain Break: £140 per person, 2 nights dinner, b&b
       Children: babies free; up to £15 thereafter (includes meals)
       Facilities: 1 cot and 1 high chair
       baby-listening system
       14 rooms, 1 family, 1 set interconnecting
       Open all year
🅿   Own car park

YORK, NORTH YORKS

Map 9

® BETTYS CAFE TEAROOMS, 6-8 St Helens Square
Tel: 01904 659 142

In the city centre.

....

The famous Bettys chain of Yorkshire tearooms and restaurants is a firm favourite of ours and has set out to cater with style for all their customers, including families.

Mothers with babies or small children can dine here with the knowledge that the Ladies offers changing facilities, a playpen and disposable nappies. There are also bibs, beakers, plates and spoons for young children, plus a 'Little Rascals' children's menu. They'll even heat up your own baby food if you ask them. There are numerous high chairs on the premises.

The main cafe-tearoom has a continental atmosphere and large picture windows that overlook St Helen's Square. A second oak-panelled tea room can be found downstairs. The Belmont Room, which was inspired by the interior decoration of the luxury liner, the Queen Mary, has recently been refurbished. It is now open for group bookings and private parties.

On Sundays the various breakfasts are very popular and you can eat at leisure, browse through the Sunday papers, and listen to the piano.

....

✗   (9am to 9pm) £2-8: Swiss rostis, Yorkshire rarebits, Swiss alpine macaroni, croutes aux champignons, club sandwiches
Children: own menu
Open every day except Christmas and New Year

🅿   Public car parks nearby

YORK, NORTH YORKS
Map 9
® LITTLE BETTYS, 46 Stonegate
Tel: 01904 622 865
In the city centre.

....

'Little Bettys' is situated in a beautiful Grade II listed building, just a stone's throw away from the Minster in the heart of Medieval York. Exotic teas and coffees from around the world are on sale in the shop, along with freshly made sandwiches and cakes to take away.

The cafe comprises four interconnected rooms with windows which overlook busy Stonegate. It's a relaxing place in which to enjoy one of the array of snacks and meals or a traditional Yorkshire afternoon tea (ham or chicken sandwiches, sultana scone with cream and a Yorkshire curd tart).

Mothers with babies can relax here since there is a separate changing room, with a shelf and changing mat and a chair. Nappies, bibs and beakers, and baby foods are also provided.

The only music to reach your ears is the occasional strains of a busker from the pedestrian precinct below.

....

✗   (9am to 5.30pm) £2-8: Swiss rostis, Yorkshire rarebits, Masham sausages, omelettes, traditional afternoon teas
Children: own menu
Open every day except Christmas and New Year
🅿   Public car parks nearby

SCOTLAND

BALLACHULISH, HIGHLAND
⊕ BALLACHULISH HOTEL
Tel: 01855 811 606
On the A828 on the south side of Ballachulish Bridge.

The hotel has a superb position alongside Loch Linnhe and is over-looked by the hills of Ben a'Bheithir. It is a grand building in the Scottish baronial style, with curved Gothic windows and pointed gables. The public rooms are just as interesting. The cocktail bar overlooks a terrace and the loch; children can have their meals in here if they wish. The restaurant sits alongside and has the same enchanting views over the loch to the hills; in the evenings you can watch the slow setting of the sun.

The bedrooms are of high quality, spacious and very comfortable, and many have the benefit of loch views.

All guests can take advantage of the excellent leisure facilities at the nearby Isles of Glencoe Hotel which also has an adventure playground.

✗   Bar meals (12pm to 9pm) £2-12
       Dinner (7pm to 9.30pm) £26
       Children: own menu, half portions
       Best Room Rate: £39 per person including breakfast
✔   Best Bargain Break: £99 per person, 3 nights - b&b
       (dinner £15)
       Children: babies free, £5 from 2 to 4, £20 from 5 to 16
       Facilities: 6 cots and 6 high chairs; baby-listening system
       54 rooms, 4 family
       Open all year, except January
🅿   Own car park

BALLACHULISH, HIGHLAND
Ⓗ ISLES OF GLENCOE HOTEL
Tel: 01855 811 602

Close to the A82, about a mile west of the village of Glencoe.

This splendid hotel is under the same ownership as the Ballachulish. It has its own distinctive style, built with a definite Scandinavian look, and has an unrivalled situation, right on the shore of Loch Leven with the dramatic pass of Glencoe behind. There are two lochside harbours and nearly two miles of water frontage, with an abundance of water sports available.

The bright, airy and comfortable bedrooms are notably spacious, and many have spectacular views of the loch. The family rooms have bunk beds in addition to doubles or singles; and most of the other bedrooms can accommodate an extra bed or a cot without strain.

The dining room, with its views over the water, reflects the relaxed style of this excellent hotel and there is also a conservatory restaurant.

A great bonus for guests is the leisure centre with its compact pool (with a steam room and a jacuzzi), paddling pool and sauna. There is a little play area off the reception area for young children, and the hotel is located in several acres of parkland. An adventure playground is situated in front of the hotel.

✗ Bar meals (10am to 10pm) £2-14
Dinner (7pm to 10pm) £22
Children: own menu, half portions
Best Room Rate: £51 per person including breakfast
✔ Best Bargain Break: £99 per person, 3 nights - b&b
Children: babies free, £5 from 2 to 4, £20 from 5 to 16
Facilities: 6 cots and 6 high chairs;
baby-listening system
39 rooms, 9 family
Open all year
🅿 Own car park

EDINBURGH, LOTHIAN
Ⓗ **THRUMS HOTEL, 14 Minto Street**
Tel: 0131 667 5545
Not far from the city centre, on the south side, off the A7.

....

The hotel is very convenient for the centre of Edinburgh and is in an area with many small hotels and guest houses. It has been constructed from two large Georgian buildings, in which many of the original features have been retained. The comfortable and well-decorated lounge has plenty of sofas and easy chairs and the large bay window gives it a bright appearance. The six family rooms have plenty of space and are attractively decorated.

An agreeable aspect of this hotel is its dining room, since part of it is housed in a conservatory, which in its turn looks out to the sizeable lawned garden with its pretty borders of flowers. It is a peaceful retreat away from the city bustle. There is also a stretch of lawned garden at the front.

....

✗   Lunch (12pm to 2pm) £8: soup, fish of the day, pudding;
      Dinner (5.30pm to 8pm) £9: prawn cocktail, roast of the day, pudding
      Children: own menu, half portions
      Best Room Rate: £30 per person
      Children: cots free; half price up to 12 years
      Facilities: 3 cots and 1 high chair,
      baby-listening
      14 rooms, 5 family
      Open all year except Christmas and New Year

🅿   Own car park

EDINBURGH, LOTHIAN
® BROWNS, 131-133 George Street
Tel: 0131 225 4422

Right in the heart of this thriving city you will find another Browns restaurant, all of whose branches make a real effort to welcome families. The interior is as welcoming as always, with potted plants in abundance, ceiling fans and strategically placed mirrors on the walls.

There are plenty of high chairs and a mother and baby room and children can park themselves anywhere in the restaurant, but not in the bar. There is loads of room in the restaurant - it can seat over 200 people - and it has the added attraction, in fine weather, of seating outside at the front of the restaurant.

✗   Food (noon to 11.30pm; until midnight on Friday and
      Saturday) £4-17: fish soup, country chicken pie, steak frites,
      vegetable tarte tatin, rack of lamb
      Children: own menu

KINCRAIG, HIGHLAND
⑤® LOCH INSH CHALETS AND BOATHOUSE RESTAURANT
Tel: 01540 651 272
Off the B9152 (it's parallel to the A9 north of Kingussie). Follow the signs to Loch Insh Watersports.

This restaurant, built from natural stone and old telegraph poles, has a superb position on the shore. Loch Insh is a great centre for water sports, including canoeing, sailing, windsurfing, raft-building and salmon and trout fishing. You can also hire mountain bikes, and there is an artificial ski slope, an adventure park and a fitness trail.

There's a grassy and sandy area by the water's edge or you can seek the shade in the woods behind where tables are also set up. Dogs are banned from the picnic area – another very sensible idea.

There's a good choice of fresh salads on the various menus (snacks, bar meals and a la carte), and the children's menu includes a drink and ice-cream. Barbecue stands are available.

There are six log cabins for hire, very well equipped and spacious and with the bonus of the beautiful surroundings. The weekly rentals vary from £200 to £710 and short breaks are available at most times of the year. Bed and breakfast ensuite is available at £17.50 per person per night.

✗   (l0am to 10pm) £1-12: filled jacket potatoes, burgers, sirloin steak, venison casserole, Loch Insh salmon
Children: own menu
Open Jan to end Oct and New Year week

🅿   Own car park

LOCHWINNOCH, STRATHCLYDE
Ⓟ **THE MOSSEND**
Tel: 01505 842 672
On the A760 close to its junction with the A737.

This roadside pub and restaurant is presentable, in its coat of pebbledash covered in white paint, and offers fine facilities for families: plenty of space inside, high chairs, a baby-changing unit, and a sizeable Fun Factory with its own soft drinks and snack bar.

That's a pretty good start and it is a congenial place for anyone, whether with a family group or not. The extensive bar area overlooks the garden and includes a lounge area at one end with a bay window. Comfortable padded settles are ranged around the walls.

At the far end you will mount a few steps to the open-plan restaurant, with its large windows. Screens of wood and coloured glass form booths, and there is a round table for eight diners in one corner. The conservatory room is a pleasant spot from which to admire the views of the distant loch and the low-lying hills.

Below there is a paved terrace and an enclosed lawned garden with a play unit and a bouncy castle.

✕　　(11.30am to 10pm) £2-8: a range of hot and cold food
　　　Children: own menu
♀　　Ale: Boddington's and guests
P　　Ample

ONICH, nr FORT WILLIAM, HIGHLAND
Ⓗ **ALLT-NAN-ROS HOTEL**
Tel: 01855 821 210　Fax: 01855 821 462
Email: allt-nan-ros@zetnet.co.uk
Website: www.allt-nan-ros.co.uk
Just east of Onich village on the A82.

Beautifully situated by Loch Linnhe, this hotel was once a Victorian manor house, and it has lovely views of the mountains and towards the Isle of Mull. You can take particular pleasure in these from the lounge and nicely decorated dining room. The bedrooms offer plenty of space, especially those with bay windows overlooking the loch.

There is a large, rambling garden at the front and the side of the hotel, and you have superb views of the loch. It has terraced lawns and trees, a stream and pond, benches and picnic tables and a shady lawn at one side.

✗   Dinner (7pm to 8.30pm) £28
       Children: own menu, half portions
       Best Room Rate: £32 per person
✔   Best Bargain Break: £150 per person, 3 nights - dinner, b&b
       Children: £5 to age 3; £10 from age 4 to 12; £20 from age
       13 to 16
       Facilities: 3 cots and 3 high chairs; baby-listening system
       20 rooms, 3 family
       Open all year except November and December
🅿   Own car park

SEAMILL, STRATHCLYDE
🅟 **WATERSIDE INN**
Tel: 01294 823 238
On the A78 just south of Seamill.

The name of this family pub and restaurant is an accurate description
of its location, alongside the waters of the Firth of Forth and with a
view to the neighbouring Farland Head. You can take a ferry from nearby
Ardrossan to the Isle of Arran.

The Waterside Inn is a sprawling roadside hostelry, with a spacious
interior and excellent amenities for all members of the family. It is
open throughout the day and serves food at all times, and has high
chairs in numbers, plus nappy-changing facilities.

The bar has a traditional pubby atmosphere, owing to the beamed
ceiling and wood panelling and the padded settles along the walls. There
is a good choice of real ales.

A large stone fireplace is a feature of the restaurant, which is
divided into three or four separate areas. There are delightful views of
the ocean from one side.

You can also enjoy the seascape from the extensive lawned garden
or from the terrace. A children's play area occupies one side of the
garden and a bouncy castle is set up in summer.

✗   (11.30am to 10pm) £2-8: a range of hot and cold food
    Children: own menu
♀   Ale: Boddington's and guests
🅿   Lots

TYNDRUM, CENTRAL
® CLIFTON COFFEE HOUSE
Tel: 01838 400 271 Fax: 01838 400 330
Email: clifton@tyndrum 12.freeserve.co.uk
On the A82.

We were delighted to list this excellent restaurant in the first edition of the *Family Welcome Guide* in 1984. We wrote then that it was 'a busy, friendly place, providing good food and facilities at very reasonable prices'. Our opinion, like their standards, has never wavered and it merited our Gold Award in 1996.

On a main tourist route, this is a busy and efficient restaurant with a craft centre and food shop which offers a wide range of products, including Scottish whisky, shortbread, preserves, cashmere, pottery and other souvenirs.

The restaurant is large, well-organized and sparkling clean. The pine ceilings, bright Formica-topped tables and many plants and flowers add to the welcoming atmosphere.

The lavatories for the disabled have shelves ideal for nappy-changing, and the owners will find a quiet spot for a mother wishing to breastfeed her baby. The staff are very happy to warm bottles and baby food.

There is an excellent range of freshly cooked food, both hot and cold, served in generous portions at reasonable prices. A good enough recommendation for anyone and especially for families on the move.

✗   (8.30am to 5.30pm) £1-7: tuna salad, fresh salmon salad,
    steak pie, kedgeree, Hebridean leek pie

Children: half portions
Closed Xmas and Boxing and New Year's days and from
January 5 to February 5
P Own car park
Disabled access

WALES

ABERAERON, CEREDIGION
® THE HIVE ON THE QUAY, Cadwgan Place
Tel: 01545 570 445
In the town centre.

....

This delightful cafe is situated on a converted coal wharf between the two harbours; the inner harbour has been pedestrianised to a large extent. Half the restaurant is in a stone building and the other half in a conservatory. You can eat in the courtyard. It is a most attractive place, amid colourful and neat cottages, and above the restaurant you will find a honey-bee exhibition. A nearby sea aquarium will appeal to the children.

All the food is freshly home-made with an emphasis on Welsh recipes; the salads are always interesting and the bread and cakes delicious (they are made from organic flour and free-range eggs). It is good to report that the children's menu is a proper offering of soup, salads and hot savoury pancakes. The honey ice creams are an absolute delight, whatever age you are, and there is also a range of honey fruit sorbets, all made from fresh fruit, and yoghurt ices.

If you wish to change a baby there is a table and chair in the Ladies.

....

✕   £4-9: fried squid, smoked haddock chowder, Tregaron pork sausage, cracked local crab and salad, whole plaice
      Children: own menu, half portions
      Open 10.30am to 5pm May, June and Sept;
      10am to 7pm July and Aug;
      closed end Sept to spring bank holiday

⚲   Ale: Theakston's
🅿   Ample street parking

ABERDOVEY, GWYNEDD
Ⓗ **HARBOUR HOTEL**
Tel: 01654 767 250
On the sea front.

....

Here is a hotel which makes a special effort to make all members of the family feel at home. It is a charming Victorian property which has been restored in a stylish and comfortable way. Amongst the nine rooms are three smart and comfortable family suites, which comprise two separate bedrooms and a bathroom. Two of these are especially quiet, since they are at the back of the hotel.

Their family restaurant, Rumbles, is open all day from 10am and offers a good range of food, including vegetarian dishes, main courses and snacks at reasonable prices. The hotel dining room is reserved for the adults in the evenings, and the basement wine bar offers an excellent choice of food, wines and beers.

....

✗   Rumbles (10am to 10pm) £2-10
        Dinner (from 7.30pm) £15
        Children: own menu, half portions
        Best Room Rate: £35 per person
✔   Best Bargain Break: 5% discount for 2 nights; 10% for 3 nights, 15% for 7 nights

Children: £5 under 3 years; £12.50 from 5 to 10; £20 from 11
to 15 years
Facilities: 3 cots and 3 high chairs;
baby-listening system
9 rooms, 3 family, 3 sets interconnecting
Open all year
P Public car park opposite hotel

ABERDOVEY, GWYNEDD
Ⓗ⑤ TREFEDDIAN HOTEL
Tel: 01654 767 213
Off the A493 half a mile north of the village.

This admirable hotel has been managed, for families, by the Cave
family for over 75 years and guests return year after year to enjoy the
friendly atmosphere and excellent facilities. The Trefeddian has an
enviable position overlooking the fine sandy beaches of Cardigan Bay,
one of which is only five minutes walk through the dunes. From the
hotel's gardens and terraces you can relax and watch the golfers on the
renowned Aberdovey golf links, which was a great favourite of the
writer Bernard Darwin.

Apart from the golf, the vast expanse of sands and the sea, there is
plenty to do at the hotel. There is a sizeable indoor swimming pool,
with a paddling pool for children, and a terrace overlooks the sea (the
area is surveyed by closed circuit television). Also indoors there is a
well-equipped playroom for young children; table tennis and a pool
table; a snooker room; and a separate lounge with a video and satellite
television.

The other facilities include an excellent all-weather tennis court
and the play area alongside has a climbing frame, swing, slide and
rockers. The children can also play in the fields beyond. Finally, there
is a nine hole pitch and putt course in front of the hotel and it is always
kept in fine condition.

The four lounges are agreeable and very comfortable and have the advantage of superb views; they include a family lounge and one for adults alongside. There is also a pleasant and quiet card room just off the reception area, with easy chairs and a selection of books.

Most of the bedrooms have been refurbished and we looked at several of the new family rooms, which are spacious enough to contain a double and a single bed, plus a sitting area with two sofa beds. From the terraces of these rooms there are delightful views across the golf course and the bay to Borth.

It is an excellent family hotel in a very pleasant seaside resort. In addition, self-catering houses are available to rent on a weekly basis from £170 to £530 a week.

Nearby: There are long stretches of beach on which to laze, and a wide choice of water sports: sailing and canoeing, wind surfing and water skiing. Railway enthusiasts have plenty to see: the Vale of Rheidol, Fairbourne and Talyllyn railways. Celtica is worth a look, as is the Corris Craft Centre. Pony trekking can be done in the vicinity, and river, sea and lake fishing are available.

✗   Lunch (12.30pm to 1.45pm) £11: wide choice including fresh
     salmon, grills and hot dish of the day, puddings and cheese
     Dinner (7.15pm to 8.30pm) £17: 5-course menu changes
     every day and includes roasts, fresh fish, vegetarian and local
     lamb dishes
     Children: high teas (from 5.30pm to 6.15pm in the restaurant),
     half portions
     Best Room Rate: £55 (dinner, b&b) per person
✔   Best Bargain Break: £110 per person, 2 nights - dinner, b&b
     Children: cots £9; extra bed £22 (includes breakfast and high
     tea or dinner)
     Facilities: 8 cots and 6 high chairs;
     baby-listening
     46 rooms, 10 family, 3 sets interconnecting
     Closed Jan/Feb
🅿   Own car park

GLYN CEIRIOG, nr LLANGOLLEN, CLWYD
Ⓗ **GOLDEN PHEASANT HOTEL**
Tel: 01691 718 281
On the B4500 west of Chirk.

....

This 18th century hotel, in the beautiful and tranquil Ceiriog Valley, is a welcoming sight. Within its grounds the hotel has its own flower-filled garden, patios, an aviary with an enclosed pool for Chinese ducks and a fish pond.

Inside, a comfortable lounge and an eating area for bar meals look down the lovely Ceiriog Valley. The splendid Pheasant Bar has dark wooden settles, stuffed game birds in glass cases, many items of militaria, an old stove with the original tiles on the fireplace surround, and a fine, carved wooden mirror. A lovely place to have the odd tincture or two.

At lunchtimes and evenings you can eat from the bar menu and the dining room offers a full menu. If you are keen on country pursuits, such as fishing and shooting, the hotel provides excellent facilities.

We looked at several family bedrooms, attractively decorated and with plenty of space. The sight of the peaceful hills from their windows was yet another bonus.

Nearby: This is a lovely part of the Border country and there are interesting castles to see at Chirk and Powis. The mansions of Erddig and Plas Newydd are worth a visit, and the Llangollen Steam Railway will take you on a trip through the delightful Dee Valley. Pistyll Rhaeadr and the Lake Vyrnwy Visitor Centre are both within easy reach.

....

✗   Bar snacks (12pm to 2.30pm and 7pm to 9pm) £3-10: lasagne, chicken in white wine, sweet & sour pork, gammon & egg;
Lunch (12pm to 2.30pm) £13: soup, grilled Ceiriog trout, bread & butter pudding;
Dinner (7pm to 8.30pm) £18: prawn & tuna salad, roast local pheasant, pudding or cheese
Children: own menu, half portions
Best Room Rate: £32 per person

✔   Best Bargain Break: £85 per person, 2 nights - dinner, b&b

Children: free up to 18 years
Facilities: 3 cots and 2 high chairs; baby-listening to all rooms
15 rooms, 5 family, 1 set interconnecting
Open all year
P Own car park

HAY-ON-WYE, POWYS
® THE GRANARY, 20 Broad Street
Tel: 01497 820 790
In the town centre.

....

The cafe is situated near the clock tower in this appealing town, whose position on the borders of England and Wales has ensured more than its fair share of mayhem over the centuries. It's peaceful enough now and the town has become a notable centre for second-hand books. There are numbers of interesting antique shops, too, and the River Wye, which meanders past the town, is a particularly alluring stretch of water.

The restaurant certainly was a granary (and also a wool collection warehouse in its time), as the machinery and pulleys which are still in place will confirm. It's a relaxed and welcoming place, with an excellent choice of freshly cooked food available, including an extensive vegetarian menu. Whenever we visit it is busy – a testament to the quality of the food and the reasonable prices.

There are several high chairs and, if you need to change or feed a baby, facilities can be made available.

....

✗ (10am to 5.30pm; until 9pm during Easter and summer holidays) £2-6: leek au gratin, rogan josh, beef in Guinness, spicy pork
Children: half portions
♀ Ale: Bass, Hancock's
P Plenty on the street except on market day (Thursday)

LLANDUDNO, GWYNEDD
Ⓗ ST TUDNO HOTEL, The Promenade
Tel: 01492 874 411
On the Promenade opposite the pier

We are firm fans of this excellent seaside hotel, which is furnished with great style and care, and welcomes all the family, from babies to grandmothers. The St Tudno sets a standard to which few hotels in the traditional seaside resorts aspire. It is not an inexpensive hotel, but it offers value for money, and is well situated opposite the pier and close to the beach, where there are donkey rides and Punch and Judy shows.

The hotel has a small heated indoor swimming pool near the coffee lounge, which, like all the public rooms, is elegantly furnished and comfortable. The Garden Room restaurant is particularly appealing, with its dashing wallpaper and hand-painted panels. It is a lovely setting in which to sample the excellent food, which has a deserved reputation for quality, based as it is on the best available local produce. Older children can join their parents for dinner, and the younger ones are served high tea in the coffee lounge at 5.45pm.

We looked at several bedrooms, all furnished and decorated in fine style and many with lovely views over the bay. The family rooms are spacious as is a luxury suite on the first floor (it has a sitting room with a sofa bed).

St Tudno is a most impressive family hotel, which is run with great style and sympathy.

Nearby: Llandudno has its own long and sandy beaches and there are many others to enjoy along the coast. The Great Orme Country Park rises nearly 700 feet from the sea and has a wide variety of wildlife. There are several castles in this part of Wales: Conwy, Penrhyn and Gwydir – and Bodnant Garden is a wonderful sight. The children will no doubt like to visit the Welsh Mountain Zoo, Gwydir Forest and the Cwm Idwal Nature Trail

✗ Bar lunches (12.30pm to 2pm): local plaice, Welsh rarebit, prawn omelette, black pudding and bacon salad, poached local salmon;

Dinner (7pm to 9.30pm) £24-£34: saddle of Welsh lamb, hot coconut and rum tart, Welsh farmhouse cheese
Children: own menu, half portions
Best Room Rate: £48 per person
✔ Best Bargain Break: from £140 per person, 2 nights - dinner, b&b and Sunday lunch
Children: £12 - £20 depending on age (including breakfast)
Facilities: 4 cots and 4 high chairs;
4 baby listening lines
19 rooms, 3 family, 2 suites
Open all year
🅿 Own car park

MAENTWROG, BLAENAU FFESTINIOG, GWYNEDD
Ⓟ THE GRAPES HOTEL
Tel: 01766 590 365
Just off the A487 as you turn into the village.

....

Wooded hills rise steeply across the road from this grey stone building dating from 1853, though there has been a hostelry on the site since the 13th century, and the ancient cellars still remain. In 'Wild Wales' George Borrow mentioned the inn and wrote that he entered 'a magnificent parlour and partook of brandy and water'.

Hanging baskets brighten the facade. At the back the large veranda, safely railed along the front, overlooks a pretty garden with shrubs and a small pond with a fountain (the garden is private).

The veranda room with its sliding window is an ideal place for summer meals and looks away to the hills. In addition, there is a sizeable family room alongside, a charming room with its stone walls, nice wooden tables and padded settles. The two bars are very appealing, with stone walls, wooden pillars and pews and a collection of pewter tankards. The whole place has a lovely atmosphere and families are made very welcome. Baby-changing facilities and three high chairs are available.

This pub is open all day and and a wide range of food is available which includes fish such as lobster, local sea bass and fruits de mer. In the afternoon during summer, cold food is available on the veranda. The accommodation at the Grapes comprises three double and three single rooms and the price for bed and breakfast is £25 per person. The old Brew House, refurbished a while ago, offers a further two units, each of which can accommodate two adults and two children.

✗   (12pm to 9.30pm) £2-15:local dressed crab, leek and ham bake, chicken korma, venison steak, supreme of pheasant
Children: own menu, half portions

♀   Ale: Bass, Boddington's, Theakston's and guests (about 30 beers are rotated)

🅿   Own car park

PENALLY, nr TENBY, PEMBROKESHIRE
Ⓗ PENALLY ABBEY HOTEL
Tel: 01834 843 033
Just off the A4139 west of Tenby.

....

This delectable 18th-century stone manor house, built on the site of an ancient abbey, sits high above the coast road and from its windows and gardens you can see Tenby golf course and Carmarthen Bay beyond. Indeed, the sandy beach is a ten-minute walk across the links (reduced green fees available).

The stone walls and gabled windows house some beautifully proportioned and spacious rooms, made even more interesting by the pointed arches of the windows and the doors; an unusual and very effective design. The highly attractive lounge has comfortable sofas and chairs, and a piano, and the elegant dining room has splendid views. The pleasant bar has a conservatory alongside which also takes advantage of the panoramic views out to sea.

If you fancy a swim, there is a small indoor heated pool; or you can relax in the five acres of mature lawns, garden and woodland. It is a lovely spot and has the added attraction of a ruined 13th-century chapel within its confines.

The owners try to keep a balance here between families and other guests, and most of the bedrooms are spacious enough to take extra beds and cots. Some of them contain sofa beds, and all the double rooms have splendid four-poster beds. We were greatly impressed by the care which has been exercised in furnishing and decorating the rooms; they are comfortable and stylish. The top floor contains two very attractive bedrooms; the double room has high wooden rafters and there is a twin-bedded room along a short corridor (plus two bathrooms). A family could use the rooms as a self-contained suite and enjoy great comfort and seclusion. The old coach house has now been converted to form four rooms, and the high standards of comfort and decoration have been maintained. Each has a four-poster bed and a bathroom, and the rooms on the upper floor have terrific views over the bay.

There are several extra facilities which are unusual and welcome; for example, breakfast is served until 10.30 in the morning. Younger

163

children (under 7) are encouraged to have their evening meals at five o'clock, so that the adults can linger undisturbed over their dinner.

The Penally Abbey is an exceptional hotel in a delightful part of Wales.

Nearby: Tenby is a busy seaside resort with sandy beaches, of which there is a wide choice, including Manorbier Bay, Barafundle Bay (owned by the National Trust) and Broad Haven. There are several castles to see: Pembroke, Tenby, Manorbier and Carew, for example; and the children will relish a visit to Manor House Wildlife Park, the Dinosaur Experience (near Tenby), Heatherton Country Sports Park, Heron's Brook Animal and Bird Park, Folly Farm, and Oakwood.

....

✗   Dinner (7.30pm onwards) £24: crab thermidor, rack of Welsh lamb, pudding or cheese
      Children: half portions
      Best Room Rate: £52 per person

✔   Best Bargain Break: 10% discount for a stay of 1 week
      Children: free to age 14
      Facilities: 3 cots and 3 high chairs;
      baby-listening system
      12 rooms, 3 family, 2 sets interconnecting
      Open all year

P   Own car park

ST DAVID'S, PEMBROKESHIRE
Ⓗ WARPOOL COURT HOTEL
Tel: 01437 720 300
Close to the centre of the town; follow the signs from Cross Square in St David's

This hotel has been recommended in the *Family Welcome Guide* since the very first edition. It is an appealing and comfortable place, built of grey stone, has extensions here and there, and was built in the 19th century as the St David's Cathedral choir school. It has a magnificent position on the unspoiled Pembrokeshire coast, adjoining stretches of which are owned by the National Trust. There are wonderful views of St Bride's Bay, especially from the large lawned garden, a delightful place to loll on a warm day, and notable for the statuary dotted around.

There are excellent facilities here, including a covered and heated swimming pool, a gymnasium, a pool table and table tennis, an all-weather tennis court, a croquet lawn and an outdoor play area for children.

The hotel has a fine reputation for its food (several awards have been won) and puts a strong emphasis on fresh local produce, especially fish: crab, lobster, sewin and sea bass are caught nearby.

✗   Bar snacks (12pm to 2pm) £4-12
        Lunch (12pm to 2pm) £16, two courses
        Dinner (7pm to 9.15pm) £34
        Children: high teas, half portions
        Facilities: cots and high chairs;
        baby-listening system
        Best Room Rate: £59 per person
✔   Best Bargain Break: £146 per person, 2 nights - dinner, b&b
        Children: free up to 14 years
        25 rooms, 6 family
        Open all year except Jan
♀   Ale: Bass
🅿   Own car park

SULLY, nr CARDIFF, GLAMORGAN
Ⓟ THE CAPTAIN'S WIFE, Beach Road
Tel: 01222 530 066
Just off the B4267

It is worth seeking out this expansive family pub merely for the views: the rocks, the seascape of Sully Bay and the island. You can lean on the sea wall and drink it in or, even better, grab a table on the terrace and enjoy it in comfort with a glass of Boddington's to sup.

The pub, long and low and painted white, has a wide frontage to the ocean and a garden to one side with an adventure playground.

Very much aimed at the family market, the interior has a number of good-sized rooms. Beyond the bar area there is a no-smoking family restaurant, which has a small play area for very young children.

Another wood-panelled room looks on to the veranda and the garden. Here also is a Charlie Chalk Fun Factory (when we visited, a children's party was in full swing) with all sorts of amusements, including a ball swamp, and the children have their own bar for soft drinks and snacks.

There is loads of room for the adults, too, including a large room beyond the bar. Up above is a spacious restaurant under the rafters.

The Captain's Wife is open all day and serves food at all times. There are plenty of high chairs, and baby-changing facilities are provided.

✗   (11.30am to 10pm) £2-8: a range of hot and cold food
     Children: own menu
♀   Ale: Boddington's and guests
🅿   Lots

166

NR WREXHAM, CLWYD
℗ THE BEECHES, Gresford
Tel: 01978 853 214
On the B5445 at Gresford, north of Wrexham.

A roadside pub on a large scale, The Beeches has become a family pub and restaurant in the Brewers Fayre chain and has a Travel Inn alongside. All the facilities required by a family are here, including high chairs, a nappy-changing unit and a children's menu; and food is available throughout the day from just before noon until 10 pm.

The capacious bar and restaurant has an array of windows on to the garden and has been constructed on a number of different levels. The various areas have cheerful wallpaper, a variety of prints on the walls, padded settles and some large bay windows. The family dining area (no-smoking) has a play area for young children, and upstairs, there is a sizeable Fun Factory and a children's soft drinks bar.

The garden is safely enclosed and has bench tables on the lawns, plus a children's play area and a bouncy castle.

✕   (11.30am to 10pm) £2-8: a range of hot and cold food
            Children: own menu
♀   Ale: Boddington's and guests
🅿   Lots

READERS COMMENTS

Please use this form to comment on any of the *Guide's* entries or to recommend establishments for future editions. The basic facilities we look for are:
- Ⓗ   hotels with cots, high chairs, and a free baby-listening service
- Ⓟ   pubs with facilities for families
- Ⓡ   restaurants with high chairs
- Ⓢ   self-catering venues with cots and high chairs

To: The Editors, *The Family Welcome Guide*, c/o Hamer Books Ltd., 3 Lonsdale Road, London SW13 9ED

Full name and address of establishment: ....
....
....
....

Phone number: ....
Comments: ....
....
....
....
....

Name and address of sender: ....
....
....
....

We regret that we cannot acknowledge these forms, but they will be properly considered

READERS COMMENTS

Please use this form to comment on any of the *Guide's* entries or to recommend establishments for future editions. The basic facilities we look for are:

Ⓗ   hotels with cots, high chairs, and a free baby-listening service
Ⓟ   pubs with facilities for families
Ⓡ   restaurants with high chairs
Ⓢ   self-catering venues with cots and high chairs

To: The Editors, *The Family Welcome Guide*, c/o Hamer Books Ltd., 3 Lonsdale Road, London SW13 9ED

Full name and address of establishment: ....
....
....
....

Phone number: ....
Comments: ....
....
....
....
....

Name and address of sender: ....
....
....
....

We regret that we cannot acknowledge these forms, but they will be properly considered

READERS COMMENTS

Please use this form to comment on any of the *Guide's* entries or to recommend establishments for future editions. The basic facilities we look for are:

- Ⓗ   hotels with cots, high chairs, and a free baby-listening service
- Ⓟ   pubs with facilities for families
- Ⓡ   restaurants with high chairs
- Ⓢ   self-catering venues with cots and high chairs

To: The Editors, *The Family Welcome Guide*, c/o Hamer Books Ltd., 3 Lonsdale Road, London SW13 9ED

Full name and address of establishment: ....
....
....
....

Phone number: ....
Comments: ....
....
....
....
....

Name and address of sender: ....
....
....
....

We regret that we cannot acknowledge these forms, but they will be properly considered

READERS COMMENTS

Please use this form to comment on any of the *Guide's* entries or to recommend establishments for future editions. The basic facilities we look for are:

Ⓗ   hotels with cots, high chairs, and a free baby-listening service
Ⓟ   pubs with facilities for families
Ⓡ   restaurants with high chairs
Ⓢ   self-catering venues with cots and high chairs

To: The Editors, *The Family Welcome Guide*, c/o Hamer Books Ltd., 3 Lonsdale Road, London SW13 9ED

Full name and address of establishment: ....
....
....
....

Phone number: ....
Comments: ....
....
....
....
....

Name and address of sender: ....
....
....
....

We regret that we cannot acknowledge these forms, but they will be properly considered